1960-2010:

GAME OVER FOR

ITALY'S MOST CRIMINAL GOVERMENTS

When a country like Italy,
was granted to the mafia from the south
to flourish for decades
to invade the north of the country
there can be no plausible excuse for a politician
to escape from the responsibility
to have contributed to the ruin of the whole country.
Today, Italy is a corrupt country
governed by the political mafia
The past speaks for itself

Adriano Giuliano

authorHOUSE®

AuthorHouse™
1663 Liberty Drive
Bloomington, IN 47403
www.authorhouse.com
Phone: 1-800-839-8640

Published by AuthorHouse   07/12/2012

ISBN: 978-1-4772-1821-1 (sc)
ISBN: 978-1-4772-1822-8 (e)

Contents

Notes on the Cover

The cover of the book may seem like nothing more than a way to attract people's attention. In my opinion, the cover should represent the soul of the book, and every writer should attempt to design his own cover. Like a painting, it should offer a visual portrayal of the author's mind. It is true—I have a lot of resentment inside of me because of the injustice happening in my country. I write because I don't know any other alternative to communicate these powerful feelings.

Introduction

A reinstatement of the Republic of Venice is in order. The Venetians must be the masters of their territory, not other ethnicities, as is the case today.

In this book I present historical facts showing how the Italian government has been hijacked by corrupt politicians, with ties to the Sicilian Mafia, the Camorra of the Campania region, and the 'Ndrangheta in Calabria.

This book is not intended to create problems for the country of Italy; Italians have done a good enough job of that by themselves over the years—both their politicians and their people. I will simply describe the facts as they happened in the past and continue to take place in the present.

You cannot force people with such different cultures to stay together under the same law while one part of the country is not respected. The people of Veneto do not deserve what is happening. Italy is in a state of great disaster, yet the Venetians have done nothing to create this great debt; in fact, they are the only ones contributing towards reducing it. Therefore, Veneto must be ruled by the Venetians, not by executives from a country with a completely different culture. I do not mean to discriminate against anyone, simply to claim the right of the Venetians to run their country, the right of any civilized people. I will state the facts as they happened in the south to illustrate the enormous cultural difference, and I will call for a referendum so that the people of Veneto can form the Venetian Republic.

The key idea of democracy is untouchable in the world today. But you rarely hear of social justice. Is democracy worth it at all costs, even the freedoms of others? *What is democracy without freedom*? I am a citizen of Veneto, compelled by an unjust historical past to be an Italian citizen. As I began to learn more about my country, I instantly discovered that I could never be part of the Italian nation. The cultural differences between northern and southern Italy are basically too broad. It must be accepted—not only in Italy but also in other parts of the world—which it is a crime against humanity to force people of different ethnic cultures to live together within the same nation. This is what began in Italy about 150 years ago. Each person has the right to live a life according to his or her desires. Nobody—I repeat, nobody—has the right to invade the territory and to impose his rule on the local people. This is what has happened in my country, and I as a citizen of Veneto, make out it as my duty to fight against the invaders. And when the invaders forced their way of life upon us, one that is different and evil, my obligation as a citizen is strengthened, and only the death will stop me in my pursuit of the Republic of Venice. For this is the only way the Venetian people will regain their dignity as a community.

ADRIANO GIULIANO

People are free to travel the world but not to conquer it; indeed, we must respect all peoples and their cultures, even those that are inherently evil, such as those in certain regions of southern Italy.

Chapter 1

Presentation of the Facts

In the past, through wars and plebiscites, the entire Italian Peninsula became one national government from north to south by the same laws. This unification did not take into account the enormous cultural diversity among its different regions—particularly the north and the south of the country. The cultural differences between Veneto and Campania are so vast that one might as well be comparing Germany to China

The unification policy enacted by the Savoy, through a plebiscite scam, ended with the annexation of Veneto. Out of 650,000 voters, only 69 were opposed to the annexation of Venice to the Kingdom of Italy. (Which leads one person to ask: when in the history of the world has there ever been such an outcome in any political election or referendum?)

If the people who sailed from Genoa with Garibaldi in 1860 had been aware of the traditions and customs of the peoples of southern Italy, these people never would have arrived in Marsala (Sicily), because they would have known they would never match. This is confirmed by recent events. The biggest supporters of Umberto Bossi's Northern League come from just upstream, from Bergamo. Many fighters who left with Garibaldi came precisely from the Bergamo valleys. Now, not only Bergamo and northern Italy but everyone is tired of the disastrous economic situation caused by the people of the south. In short, uniting people with completely different ways of thinking and conceiving of civil life has done nothing but create problems for both people.

Who will marry having never known the bride or the groom, committing to making that person a part of their life forever? There is no require for a united Italy, or for that matter a united Europe, but there is need for a united *world*, in which thousands of culturally diverse people are respected, which unfortunately has never been the case in Italy. Fortunately, there is a possibility of divorce. I turn to you, Veneto people, so that you may regain your dignity as a people, not to be a slave to Rome.

Compatriot Venetians, the Venetian Republic made history in the past, not many centuries ago. Now our country is reduced to a state of subjugation, as it was 2000 years ago. Rome today finds all its leaders in the south. The police, *carabinieri*, Guardia di Finanza, Army, and so on all come from the south. Just like 2000 years ago. It seems that our lot as Venetians is to just work and to pay taxes to Rome. There are thousands of people who hold managerial positions without being capable to manage them. They reached those powers there only because they have political clout, and they damage everything they touch. Just think of the airline Alitalia. In the past decade have suffered losses of more than 2 billion Euros. However, Alitalia's chief executive earned twice that of the CEO of Air France, a money-spinning company.

Even elementary and public school teachers, university professors, and government officials all of them come from the south. Are we the citizens of Veneto all so stupid and ignorant that we cannot turn out our own public officials and teachers? Is it reasonable that, in the name of democracy and national unity, a minority people must endure such humiliation? If it were true that the south had the best professors, managers, workers, and specialists, there would be nothing to complain about. Yet many people from the south simply do not perform their jobs in a proper way.

Just think of the many people in northern Italy that were not able to graduate from their postsecondary school programs but moved to the south and graduated with no difficulty. For example, the current Minister of Public Administration, Ms Gelmini, from Brescia, moved to Catanzaro (Calabria) to graduate. When a journalist recently asked her the reasons why, she replied that in those days it was difficult to graduate in Brescia. Even those who cannot get a driver's license move to the south for a couple of months so they can obtain their license. The last news I heard: a person who could not get a disability pension moved to Crotone (Calabria region), where he got one easily.

These are things I know already, but the witness of other journalists and writers will likely enhance the reader's opinion of this book. Therefore, I present my witnesses, whose books have been published in Italy:

1. La deriva. perchè l'Italia rischia il naufragio. by Stella & Rizzo 2008
    The drift—because Italy, in danger of sinking.
2. L'inferno. profondo sud-male oscuro. by Giorgio Bocca 1992
    The hell. deep South—dark evil
3. LA FIERA DELLE SANITA'. Politici corrotti. Medici cialtroni.
    Imprenditori rapaci. Criminali e burocrati. Un giro d'affari da 100 miliardi di euro. Tra abusi, truffe e disservizi, ecco chi mette in pericolo la salute degli italiani. by Daniela Minerva 2009
    THE HEALTH FAIR. Corrupt politicians. Medical charlatans.
    Entrepeneurs of prey. Criminals and bureaucrats. A turnover of 100 billions euros. Among abuses, fraud and inefficiency, that's who endangers the health of italians.
4. SANGUISUGHE. Le pensioni d'oro che ci prosciugano le tasche.
                                            by Mario Giordano (reprint) 2011
    LEECHES. Gold Pensions that drain your pockets.

HERE ARE A FEW NOTES ABOUT THE AUTHORS OF THE BOOKS LISTED ABOVE

1. Gian Antonio Stella was born in 1953 in Asolo, near Treviso (Veneto region) columnist for the newspaper "Corriere della Sera". He has written several books including the bestsellers "The Caste. So Italian politicians have become untouchables" in 2007. Sergio Rizzo was born in 1956 in Ivra (Piedmont region) is responsible for compilation of the Roman sconomica 2Corriere della Sera newspaper. "He has also worked for other newspapers as" Milano Finanza "and" Il Giornale ". He has written books, of which two with Gian Antonio Stella.

2. Giorgio Bocca was born in 1920 in Cuneo (Piedmont region) and died in Milan in 2011. It was the most loved and read journalist of Italy, although in recent times highly critical of the south. He participated in the partisan war as commander in the formation of "Justice and Freedom". But it was in the 60s that he began his knowledge of the South as a special envoy. In 1975 he was among the founders of the famous newspaper "La Repubblica" in which he worked as a columnist. Leads the heading "The 'anti-Italian" on the weekly "L'Espresso". He wrote many books, including the most famous "The Hell. Deep South—Evil Dark". Very hard on the speech RAITRE at 8.30 pm, the program Fabio Fazio. He criticized the city of Naples, calling it a cimiciaio (meaning full of bugs), and full of people of ill repute. The journalist who criticized this statement by reminding him that he should be grateful to Naples, because he wrote a book about Naples, precisely because the city is so. Mr. Bocca answered: ""Grateful? As if to say: I am grateful because I go to big game hunting of wild beasts. In short, do not you grateful to the beasts, that give you the opportunity to do what you want to do (write), and I'm supposed to fraternize with the beasts."

3. Daniela Minerva was born in 1958 in Bologna. She's the responsible for medical and health pages of the weekly "L'Espresso". Author of several books, the most famous is specifically "the fair of healthcare."

4. Mario Giordano was born in 1966 in Alessandria (Piedmont). And he is a columnist for the newspaper "Il Giornale" and he directed "News Mediaset" on Berlusconi's private TV Channel 5. And he is the author of several books about the immorality of the Italian people.

Any reasonable person who does not know the history of Italy can just read any two of these books to understand the huge cultural differences between the people of the north and south.

It's not fair to force a people to be subjected to another people. We know very well that in multiethnic societies, only the most cunning and mischievous will obtain important positions in the society. The North of Italy is the classic laboratory in which you can see the truth of what I am saying.

Since the early 50s, thanks to the economic boom, tens of thousands of people from the south to the north. In the following years industrial cities such as Milan, Turin, and Genoa were so flooded that in a few short years local citizens became a minority. And when they came, they were placed in positions of authority without regard to merit by their friends and family. This quickly led to a sense of entitlement among southerners, who came to believe that they deserved high social positions without working for it. This happened not only in the private sector but in the public sector as well. In short, southern people outright invaded the entire north of the country.

My country, the Veneto region, is still mostly composed of Venetians, but, unfortunately, in almost all state agencies, management and workers are from southern Italy.

Infrastructure is another area that has suffered greatly. In their book, journalists Stella and Rizzo wrote a chapter entitled "Infrastructure, from the First one to the Last one". They described how the first freeway in the world, the Milan-Varese (50 km long) was built in northern Italy in 1924 in under a year. The Littorio Bridge (now the Liberty Bridge), almost 4 km long, which connects Venice to the mainland, was inaugurated on 25 April 1933, by Mussolini after only two years of work. From the advent of Fascism until the late 60s, Italy was great nation of public works projects. But after the 60s arrogant politicians and invading southerners gave us the country we have now: a country that is backwards when it comes to infrastructure, a country with an incompetent and corrupt ruling class (comprised mostly of people from the south).

Education has also faltered. In the book, [La deriva. perchè l'Italia rischia il naufragio], by Stella and Rizzo, according to OCSE(Organisation for Economic Co-operation and Development) statistics, Italian students are among the last in Europe, thanks to the students of southern Italy. Yet hardly anyone in the world is as ignorant as the Sicilian fifteen-year-old (as journalist Salvo Intravia laments in the newspaper *La Repubblica*). Students in Friuli-Venezia Giulia are among the most talented in the world, and young Venetian and Lombard students are above the international average, but the south brings down the over all score. This has much to do with the training of the teachers. For years, those who have failed to graduate in northern Italy have moved to the south and got their degree there. What could you expect from such a system? Can any country expect to have trained teachers and students with systems so disingenuous? We have just learned that Sicilian students are among the worst in the world, yet only 1.3 per cent fail out of school. In many Calabria schools, none are failed at all.

What mostly makes me angry is the fact that the regions of northern Italy must endure the ineptitude and arrogance of southerners in their civil service. I was so heated when I went to get my passport at the police station in Verona. There was not a single person there with a Venetian accent. Let's get one thing straight: to the people of Veneto the people of the south are complete foreigners. So then, should the people of Veneto adapt to the corrupt culture of the south, in the name of democracy and national Italian unity? What are the social values that we should learn from these people?

Italy's Artful Dodger

The current President of the Republic, Giorgio Napolitano, believes he knows better than we Venetians about the culture of southern Italians. He has the courage to respond to the voters of the Northern League that fiscal federalism makes good sense. Unfortunately, no one has the heart to answer this claim. Not a single journalist was brave enough to stand up to Dodger Napolitano and ask the tough questions. An honest person would have asked this simple question: "Mr President, for more than forty years, the southern regions have received huge funding, without showing any profits. In fact, the south has had more resources than countries like England, France, and Germany. Even after fifty years, there have been no results. How comes that you ask for more money from the north to maintain such a lazy and wasteful region?"

Napolitano's has answered his critics, "You cannot change the constitution which cost a lot of blood." But in fact, dear Napolitano, when it comes in order to improve people's lives, everything can change. The only thing that cannot be changed is the death, because when your time comes, there's nothing you can do.

Since 1955, Napolitano has been continually elected to the Chamber of Deputies in the Italian Communist Party, with its constituency in the city of Naples. Now I make a simple question: if anyone of you had been elected in the city of Naples continuously since 1955, would you have forgotten your constituents? Napolitano chooses to be deaf and blind to the fact that his city remains in the hands of the Camorra (organized crime). He was deaf and blind to the fact that for decades, his Naples has been filling up with junk. How can we assume that Giorgio Napolitano is looking out for the interests of the people of northern Italy when he does not even support his fellow citizens? Every person in his place would have called for the intervention of the army in the 70s to clean up the streets of the Camorra. None of this was done. For him "hammer and sickle" have always been more important than the people.

Shame on you, Mr President. Although, as many people from the south, you have no idea about shame. I wonder, dear Mr President, where do you find the courage to travel around the world representing Italy when you have left your own countrymen in the hands of organized crime for decades? If you as a deputy really cared about your people rather than "hammer and sickle code", you would have called for the involvement of the army. The Red Brigade and other terrorist criminal organizations have been defeated in the past. I do not understand why the Camorra cannot be defeated in the same way. Well, the Italian State easily defeated terrorist groups in the 80s, yet now we find ourselves unable to put down criminal organizations of the south.

Obviously you did not possess the will determination to go up against organized crime, which has controlled the vote for decades in many southern regions.

5

Where there is a will, there is a way.

The Southern Character

In general, the people of the south are mischievous, domineering, and arrogant. When these people have a shred of power, they protect it at all costs. The writer Giorgio Bocca explains this in his famous book, L'inferno—profondo sud-male oscuro (*The hell—deep south—dark evill)*. I learned a lot reading this book. More than forty years ago, Mr Bocca had experience of life in the south as a correspondent of the newspaper *La Stampa* of Turin. He outlined the southern character in great length and breadth. After hearing of this book I ordered it via the Internet, and I ate it up in a few days' time, then reread it many times. Why Mr Bocca, describes his experience of life in the south, as a correspondent of the newspaper. His writing is simple and elegant, and I recommend all Venetians read it, as it is imperative for the people of northern Italy to know the cultures of others. If I had had the chance to read this when I attended middle school, I would have dealt much differently with Professor Riggio, my first year schoolmaster.

The first person from the south who behaved wickedly with me was Professor Riggio, a woman from Calabria. She taught Italian, Latin, and History during my first year of middle school. One day she gave us an exercise, asking us to argue the position that work ennobles man. In my paper, I expressed ideas that differed from those of the teacher. I stated that while it is good to feel honoured and happy to do one's job, millions around the world perform hard, unhealthy work for which they are paid little. Was there some great sin in describing this harsh reality? These views were very different from what she was teaching, and so I became her biggest enemy. Naïve as I was, I took no notice. I was the stereotypical young liberal. I would never have imagined that my professor would fail me merely for expressing my views, particularly as I got good grades the year before. I remember my shock when, after exams, I saw my name posted on the wall next to the office door with the word "fail" written beside it The professor Riggio come out from the office with a sly smile and she said, "Adriano, repeat the year. If you want it, you can do it." At the time, I accepted her words as a mercy. I left school and went to work. I travelled around the world, returning to Italy when I was thirty-seven.

How damn stupid I was! Now that I know the southern culture, I realize that those few words, along with that smile, representative victory for her over me and my culture. She succeeded in making me believe I was not good enough to continue with my studies. If at the time I knew the character of southern people, as I know now, I never would have contradicted the Professor Riggio. I would have told her what she wanted to hear, and my life today would be much different.

By what right did this professor seek to ruin my life? To change my destiny? I was good at school! Anne Frank said, "I believe in human goodness." I would add, "I also believe in human wickedness." However, the past is gone. Now we must think of future generations. This includes making sure that bad people do not concentrate in places of power.

Pointing out evil by describing cruel events is not discrimination. Indeed, it is a civic and moral duty that all citizens should practise. People behaviour must be stopped, not allowed to propagate. People have a right to know what's going on and judge whether it is right or wrong.

A Culture of Criminals

It's a sad comment that the leaders of all public bodies come from the most corrupt regions of the country. And it is *inhuman* that the same leaders have permitted hundreds of criminals to be transferred from the south to the north in the name of national unity. In any other normal country, these people would be in prison.

From the 60s onwards, Italy has allowed southern criminals to occupy our country. With the law of "stay obligato", criminals have been transferred from southern regions to northern ones by police orders. As a result, major crime organizations have invaded northern Italian cities, regions that previously did not know, such as bullying, arrogance, and cruelty. Since the 60s, various Italian governments have encouraged these criminal groups in this way. *This is a crime against the people of northern Italy.*

Worse yet, not only were these criminals transferred to the north, but they were given jobs.

This is not to mention white-collar crime. As Italy continues to control excessive tax evasion in this country, we are learning that in many areas of the south, there are thousands of workshops unknown to the government. This is the way things function in southern Italy, and we have known about it for decades, why has no political party ever stood up against this practise?

I cannot understand why not a single politician in all those years is questioned and the practises in Parliament.

There are many wolves among the sheep in Italy.

The Facts

Italy has always been governed primarily by corrupt and evil people—it is a fact.

Southern Italy has had huge amounts of money to create growth and employment—it is a fact.

Southern Italy that has used these resources to enjoy life—it is a fact.

That the head of the Italian state, Giorgio Napolitano, will continue to seek resources to develop the south and to insult the people of northern Italy—it is a fact. George continues to say, "Padania does not exist and there are no Padano people."

The EC requested the return of 700,000 Euros from a town near Naples, because the money was spent to pay for an Elton John concert instead of being used as it was intended—it is a fact.

Using money intended for development to put on a concert? That's why the south has not developed.

For decades, local politicians have been siphoning of funds intended for development of the territory, leaving crumbs for the people. Honest politicians would build roads, bridges, and homes for the people, would have developed agriculture and tourism. The south of Italy is a beautiful country—it's the people that ruin it. That's not to say that all the people of the south are evil, just that there are *too many* of them are. It's all too easy to blame the politicians only. Yet if criminal organizations proliferate, it is because thousands of people join them. In which civilized country can people be arrested for Mafia crimes, then released after a few years, following the expiry of the terms of custody? In southern Italy, too often, hardened criminals are released in this way.

A very dear English friend told me years ago, "Every country gets what it deserves." Quite right, but this is not the case in the Veneto region, which, along with other northern regions, has not added to the debt but has helped to reduce it.

There is no point blaming Berlusconi. He is merely the product of rotten and corrupt society. Had Berlusconi been born in Denmark, certainly he would not have committed all those crimes for which he has been accused, for the simple reason that in that country he would not have been given the opportunity to commit such crimes. So please, gentlemen of the left (Bersani and company), stop acting like saints, because after the war, you were playing politics as well, gentlemen ex-communists.

You are all guilty, to have built a country so rotten and corrupt. As in the universe, in life nothing happens by chance—there is always a cause, a trigger event.

The Way Forward

I, as an ordinary Venetian citizen, believe it is the right of my people to decide on their own future according to its own culture and ideals. This is not about disuniting Italy. It is about restoring lost dignity for affected populations, of which Veneto is one.

I turn to you, international organizations that defend the rights of ethnic minorities. Read through this book: check the veracity of what I wrote, and once we see that I have written only the truth, it is then your duty to contact international community and compel them to the referendum I propose. The Venetian people must have the right to choose whether to be part of Italy or to found the Venetian Republic. The Venetian people are tired of being a slave to Rome. They are tired of having foreign masters. They want to be the master of their own home. They want independence.

As for you, the Venetian people, it's time to open your eyes and see reality for what it is. I recommend reading the book written by Giorgio Bocca, l'inferno-profondo sud—male oscuro (The Hell. Deep South-Dark Evil). On 13/14 April 2008, elections there were 158 political symbols to choose from. This is proof enough that there are cultural differences in the country. It is not fair that the hardest, most overbearing; most arrogant people occupy positions of power in our home. Venetians, take back your territory. And regain your dignity as a people. Once you have obtained permission to hold the referendum, forget all your ideas of unity, which, as we have seen, never solved our biggest problem. Let us live as a people, with own traditions and culture.

We still have time to clean up our territory.

Unfortunately, the north has assimilated much of the unfair behaviour from the south. Dear fellow Venetians, do you really believe that such activities will lead to better lives?

Certainly no. So, all together, let's eradicate all the political parties and vote to found the Venetian Republic, in which politicians, senior civil servants, teachers, etc., are Venetian.

Let us have only two political parties. When they are too many this causes damage, as they blame each other and confuse the people. If there are only two, it's easy to know who is to blame if things are going bad.

Fellow citizens Venetians, in the coming years Italy are destined to become a very poor country. According to the OCSE, Italy is the twenty-fifth most honest country in Europe, after Bulgaria and Romania. (The northern European countries are the most honest.) There are even third world countries surpassing Italy in social honesty. This is mainly due to post-war governments. If from the 50s onward Italy had honest politicians (as in Denmark, Sweden, Norway, etc.), the country would not be in this difficult economic situation.

You must be absolutely realistic and accept the picture of the facts. With these facts before us, all we can do is accepting the damages suffered, draw up our strength as Venetians, and break away from this beautiful and damned country, Italy.

Chapter 2

A Brief History of the Three Major Political Parties and Major Italian Politicians from 1950 to 1992

Table 2.1 Main Italian Political Parties and Their Percentage of the Popular Vote

Christian Democracy

Year	House	Senate
1948	48.5	48.1
1953	40.1	40.7
1958	42.4	41.2
1963	38.3	36.5
1968	39.1	38.3
1972	38.7	38.1
1976	38.7	39.3
1979	38.3	38.3
1983	32.9	32.4
1987	34.3	33.6
1992	29.7	27.3

Italian Communist Party

Year	House	Senate
1948	31	30.8
1953	22.6	20.6
1958	22.7	21.8
1963	25.3	25.2
1968	26.9	30
1972	27.1	28.1

1976	34.4	34.2
1979	30.4	31.4
1983	29.9	30.8
1987	26.6	28.3

Italian Socialist Party

1948	31	30.8

Italian Socialist Party Together with the People's Democratic Front Party

Year	House	Senate
1953	12.6	11.9
1958	14.2	14.1
1963	13.8	14
1968	14.4	15.2
1972	9.6	10.7
1976	9.6	10.3
1979	9.8	10.3
1983	11.4	11.3
1987	14.2	13.9
1992	13.6	13.5

In addition to these three major parties in the First Republic there were fourteen other parties. Still these three parties were mainly responsible for the spread of criminal organizations in the north. If, together, they had fought criminal organizations in the south, the history of Italy would have been much different. Instead, too many politicians in the south allied themselves with the criminal Mafia, strengthening these organizations. Mafias, like a cancer, will spread if not fought at the place of origin. Therefore, you cannot help but identify the Christian Democracy, Communist Party, and Italian Socialist Party as the parties mainly responsible for the current economic situation in Italy.

How can a country so rotten demand respect from other countries? We must put aside our pride and look at reality as it is. I, as a Venetian citizen, am not sorry to say that I am still naive, because regrettably it is the truth, and I am ashamed. In

11

northern Italy there is the Mafia as well, but it originates from the south and is made up by people from southern Italy.

In this chapter I will identify the assorted political leaders of these parties, whom I accused to be colluded with criminals. I will list only the worst in terms of corruption. It would be an impossible task trying to list the all of them.

I apologize in advance to those who only see their name in the book and not names of other corrupt people, like them. I do not intend to write a thorough account of the Italian disaster, because to do so would be to write an impressive book.

Here there is some information in order to understand the terms that you will find in the book

-   In Italy there are three degrees of judgment if the defendant or the prosecutor are not satisfied with the decision of first instance, you can use with another judgment (Appeal), then there is the third instance (Cassation).
-   The prescription in criminal law determines the extinction of an offense as a result of the passing of a certain period of time. The purpose of the provision is that, after a long time by the fact, is less than both the state's interest in punishing the relevant conduct, both the need for a process of social reintegration of the offender, then you'll often find the terms prescription or prescribe.
-   This proof that all Italian governments of the past until now, have in their DNA, the culture of crime otherwise for offenses against the state, definitely should not exist, the law of "PRESCRIPTION". This law is the mother of corruption, made especially by politicians for politicians so that they can steal in every way possible without any problems. The law of PRESCRIPTION costs to the country Italy every year 60 billion Euros. So I feel compelled to reiterate that all Italian political parties are guilty of the misfortunes of the Italians
-   In 1992 he became famous the term Pool of Mani Pulite (pool of Clean Hands), which were part of public prosecutors in Milan: Antonio Di Pietro, Gerardo D'Ambrosio, Francesco Saverio Borrelli, Ilda Boccassini, Gherardo Colombo, Piercamillo Davigo and Armando Spataro, which, with their investigations decimated the major political parties of the Italian Christian Democrats and the Italian Socialist Party.

Christian Democracy

The Christian Democrats were founded in 1942, inspired by Christian Democrats. The founders of the party, including Alcide De Gasperi, comprised people of the dissolved Italian Popular Party. From 1943 until the end of the war, in 1945, even the DC had its partisan brigades, although the Communists were in the majority. Although both fought against fascism, when they met each other to have a drink or to eat something, they always had a gun under the table.

I still remember the story my aunt told me abou t the priests who went around the whole of Italy to induce people to vote for Christian Democrats. It was well known at the time that communism preached atheism, so priests and communists were bitter enemies then. Many priests were killed when the war ended. Famous was the "triangle of death" between the cities of Modena, Bologna, and Reggio Emilia. Emilia Romagna still enjoys the reputation of being a communist region, and in that accursed triangle dozens of seminarians and priests were killed. Perhaps it was ignorance or maybe it was just the times to have hardened the hearts of criminals like that.

Immediately after the war, political competition was tough between the two major parties, the Christian Democrats—supported by the United States, who wanted to make a free and democratic society—and the Italian Communist Party, supported by the Soviets. Fortunately, the DC won.

On 2 June 1946, there was a referendum in which people were asked to choose between monarchy and republic. The people decided for the republic. From 1946 to 1948 the Christian Democrats, in the Constituent Assembly, was able to involve all the other parties. It was a great item to see that in the Constituent Assembly, but it also bolstered the Communists. Together, in eighteen months the parties wrote the "Constitution of the Italian Republic."

The major DC party leaders, as well as De Gasperi, included Amintore Fanfani, John Gronchi, Antonio Segni, John Leone, Aldo Moro, Giulio Andreotti, Arnaldo Forlani, Francesco Cossiga, Oscar Luigi Scalfaro, and Ciriaco De Mita, as well as others, would be involved in corruption scandals or even worse.

In the mid-50s policies were set that expressed the different political orientations of the parties. The year 1968 was the beginning of the Cultural Revolution, to which policy had to adapt. Young people wanted extra freedom and additional rights, which in those years they thought meant unions, especially the CGIL union, which had communist leanings.

The DC had to give given on many issues, especially requests for wage increases demanded by the unions. The mid-70s gave birth to the first terrorist organizations, such as the Front Line, the Red Brigades, the Revolutionary Armed Nuclei, and other groups. On 16 March 1978, Aldo Moro, the leader of the DC, was seized by the Red Brigades. His five police escorts were killed. He was held prisoner by the Red Brigades for fifty-five days, during which time he was tried by the communist terrorists. He was allowed to write letters to family members as well as government politicians. The media at the time encouraged the government not to give into any demands in exchange for these prisoners, including the release of imprisoned terrorists. Failing to obtain the release of their comrades, the terrorists decided to kill Moro, and on 9 May his corpse was found in the boot of a Renault on Via Michelangelo Caetani, not far from Via delle Botteghe Oscure, where the Italian Communist Party is headquartered in Rome.

Those were the days of the famous "historic compromise" between DC and the Communist Party. But its main proponent, now dead, could speak no more of that compromise.

Christian Democrats, from the postwar period until the Tangentopoli scandal of 1992, again in conjunction with other parties, was in power. One thing is certain: DC began well after the war, but in the 1960s its politics degenerated. There were many reasons for this. Many who sought money for the party actually used it to enrich themselves. There were those in the south who allied with criminal gangs to get votes and get rich. There was also a lack of strict rules. All this led to the ruination of Italian political parties and politicians themselves.

There were many Democratic politicians involved in corruption, or worse, from the 60s onwards. The link between the rise of terrorist organizations and the collusion and social injustice perpetrated by DC was clearly visible to all intelligent people. The memory of Giorgio Almirante still resonates within me. On television programs, when the Christian Democrats were accused of stealing, his response was always the same: "Shut up, fascist." When a person responds this way, it means he no longer knows how to defend himself from being accused of theft. I was young then, and I knew little or nothing about policy, but I will always remember that usual words against Mr Almirante: "Shut up, fascist."

Giulio Andreotti
Born in Roma, 1919
Lazio region

7-times Chairman of the Board
8-times Minister of Defense
5-times Foreign Minister
3-times Minister for State Holdings
2-times Finance Minister
2-times Minister of the Budget
2-times Minister of Industry
1-time Minister of Interior
1-time Minister of the Treasury
1-time Minister of Cultural Heritage
1-time Minister of Community Policies

The "Beelzebub of Italian Politics". This is just one of his nicknames in this country. Uncle Julius is another, given to him by the Mafia. He is one of the main culprits of the existing state of affairs in this country.

In 1993, the current attorney general of Turin, Mr Gian Carlo Caselli, was an anti-Mafia prosecutor in Palermo. This was the year he began the investigation that led to the Andreotti trial. The trial ended 15 October 2004, with the charges of criminal association being dropped because of prescription

Andreotti was appointed senator for life by Francesco Cossiga (when he was president of the Republic). Andreotti In the process of Palermo, on charges of being the largest political reference of Cosa Nostra (the Sicilian Mafia) on the island, through the democratic politician and senator Salvo Lima. In 2002, the Senator was condemned to twenty-four years with the incarceration since he was incriminated of instigating the murder of journalist Mino Pecorelli. Pecorelli was close to publish an extremely embarrassing article about the Prime Minister Giulio Andreotti, entitled "The Allowances of the President". Unluckly multiple gunshot wounds killed the journalist. on the evening of 20th March 1979, Further evidence of his misdeeds is provided by lawyer Gianfranco Rosini (a friend of Pecorelli), who, in an interview published in a newspaper(il Corriere della sera) in 1993, declared that Pecorelli confided that he considered Andreotti one of the greatest criminals of the recent history of the Italian Republic.

On November 17th, 2002, the Court of Appeal convicted Andreotti to twenty-four years in prison, imposed by a court in Perugia, than on October 2003 the Court of Cassation annuls the judgment of indictment, recognizing him innocent.

Mafia snitch Gaspar Mutolo said that the murder of Salvo Lima on march 12 1992, was a warning that the Mafia boss wanted to send to Andreotti, just about the first maxi trial against Cosa Nostra, The process of Palermo was named "Maxi Trial", because you were involved more than 400 mobsters, and began in February 1986 and ended December 16, 1987. It was the first time that mafia organization "Cosa Nostra" had such a great process, condemning many of its affiliates.

Andreotti, and politicians of the Christian Democrats of the island, no longer had the political strength to continue to protect the Mafia, which, unfortunately, did not understand, because after the Maxi Trial, numerous homicides was committed in Sicily by the mafia.

Another repentant, Francesco Marino Mannoia, is still one of the main witness of the accusation against Giulio Andreotti. The Mafia in Mannoia killed his mother, sister, and aunt. Leonardo Messina signed the minutes in which he declared that Giulio Andreotti was affiliated with the Cosa Nostra. These confessions led to the arrest of more than 200 people in the Italian Mafia.

Here we should also mention the murder of Christian Democrat leader Piersanti Mattarella (President of the Sicilian Region), who decided to clean up the DC Sicilian and was set to collide with Mr Rosario Nicoletti. Nicoletti (according to the testimony of Marino Mannoia) declared the goodness of that murder. The boss of Cosa Nostra, Stefano Bontade, after having met with Andreotti, decided to remove the obstacle Mattarella, and on 6th January 1980, the President of the region was killed in Palermo, Sicily. Rosario Nicoletti failed to change his mind. After many years, Franco Evangelisti, Andreotti's secretary, said, "After Mattarella's murder, I asked what he thought of Salvo Lima, and he simply replied, 'When we set up agreements are establish they should be maintained.' In conclusion: the physical evidence is more than enough to say that

Andreotti, if not a Mafia member, was a great criminal, perhaps the greatest that Italy had seen since the war. Andreotti entertained "friendly relations" with the Mafia bosses, asking them for special treatments and showing a willingness to reciprocate. Even put in a good word to prevent Piersanti Mattarella from being killed, but when those negotiations fell through he failed to denounce those responsible for the murder of the President Region of Sicily.

They wrote that the judges of the Supreme 15 October 2004 confirmed the decision previously issued by the Court of Appeals charged Andreotti: acquittal for lack of evidence for the offense of criminal association (art. 416bis: this article came into force after 1980, and worsens the position of the accused by adding "Mafia") and prescribed for the offense of criminal association (art. 416), whose life senator would have had dealings with the Mafia until 1980, before the murder, the January 6, 1980, of the President of the Region Mr. Piersanti Mattarella.

The relationship between Andreotti and the Cosa Nostra is entirely clear. Senator Andreotti was fully aware that his political contacts in Sicily (the senator Lima, the Salvo cousins and later the political Ciancimino) entertained friendly relations with some Mafia bosses. Andreotti cultivated friendly relations with the same boss, who had revealed to the same availability and a substantial assistance on concessional terms; the mafia bosses that they had asked favours, and that they had met to discuss about it.

Andreotti tried to convince the boss Bontade, not to kill the president of the Sicilian region Mattarella, but to give him only a warning, unfortunately without success, because, Mattarella was killed without mercy.

The President of the court during the process, made a strong criticism about the Mattarella's murder, because according to him, Andreotti should have alerted Mr. Mattarella of the danger he was running going against the mafia interests, and especially to warn the prosecutor's office in Palermo, so that it was given protection. But he did nothing to save the life of the Regional President Mr. Mattarella.

For three decades, the church had been spreading good promotion among the people of Sicily so they would vote for the Christian Democrat Andreotti. The discovery that Andreotti and Sicilian politicians of his party had been in collusion with the Mafia for thirty years failed to raise an objection among the prelates of the church. Indeed, the even comforted him jerking his trial in Palermo, even though more than thirty-five people accused him. In such a corrupted country corrupt, you can expect everything.

For example, so you can understand how little respect this senator for life had for the people of northern Italy, Giorgio Bocca writes, "And so, in the last government of Andreotti (1991) was not a single minister of Emilia-Romagna, one of the richest regions of Italy, and most advanced, but there was a large group of ministers and undersecretaries of Campania: Gava, Pomicino, Scotti, Di Lorenzo, Mannino, Mastella,

Vito, Del Mese, Ciampaglia, Santonastaso, Francesco De Lorenzo (know in Italy as "Healt King" because involved in bribes when he was minister of the italian health) not counting the President of the Christian Democrat Ciriaco De Mita."

Note:

The Campania is one of the most corrupt regions of Italy, known worldwide for his powerful criminal organization called "Camorra", which imposes its law in the city of Naples. The collusion of politicians with the Neapolitan Camorra has been known for decades, in fact, no politician gets votes in Naples without the consent of the Camorra.

Giorgio Bocca also writes, "A colleague of mine said to me, 'Do not accuse them (politicians) in your articles. They are gangsters. You will be doing them a favor. The fame of being a gangster here (in Napoli) will get you votes.'"

Arnaldo Forlani
Born in Pesaro, 1925
Marche Region

1-time Chairman of the Board
1-time Vice-Chairman of the Board
1-time Foreign Minister
1-time Minister of Defense

In 1992, at the beginning of Operation Clean Hands, Forlani was involved with Enimont. Enimont was the giant of the Italian chemical industry in the 90s, counting financier Raul Gardini as a member. Gardini paid bribes to politicians and entrepreneurs, about 150 billion lire in total, in order to get out of Enimont without a serious loss of money. Forlani was one of the politicians to be bribed, and on 21 January 1998, he was convicted to 2 years and 4 months imprisonment by the Supreme Court.

Of course, as always in Italy, Mr Forlani did not serve his sentence in jail but was given to social services, and working for Caritas of Rome until the end of the sentence.

Current UDC party leader Pier Ferdinando Casini was Forlani's spokesman.

Ciriaco De Mita
Born in Nusco, 1928
Campania region

1-time Chairman of the Board

This gentleman, with amnesty in 1990, blew the whistle on "Tangentopoli" (meaning bribery), which started in 1992 with the arrest of Mario Chiesa, the president of a nursing home who pocketed a bribe of 7 million lire. Since the beginning, the "clean hands" pool of the Court of Justice in Milano, made sure that all political parties were udes to take bribes. That's Italy. An official pardon should not exist for such offenses; however, it was exactly the huge general amnesty, which allowed them to do not change the road.

It was also found that De Mita gained a significant amount of money thanks to the 1980 earthquake that hit Irpinia. He, along with other relatives, was a member of the National Bank of Irpinia, which was greatly improved thanks to the earthquake. This happened in 1988, when judges set aside significant amounts of money for rebuilding, which passed through the bank.

Antonio Gava
Born Castellamare di Stabia, 1930
Campania region
Died Roma, 2008
1-time minister of finance
1-time minister of interior

Elected for the first time as a deputy in 1972 with the Christian Democrats, Antonio Gava was one of the most powerful men of the Christian Democrats in the Campania region, earning the nickname "viceroy" for his great ability to get votes.

The courts of Naples prosecuted him for maintaining relationships, through other characters, with the Camorra (organized crime). In 1993 he was sentenced in the first two levels of jurisdiction for receiving stolen funds. The Supreme Court was taken up the case. Even at the beginning of 1993, according to some friends, Gava went through quite the ordeal, with the arrest, his jail term, then house arrest. The charge was "Mafia association" with regards fake votes during the election time. He was under house arrest for about 7 months before he was finally acquitted in 2006 "due to lack of appeals."

Despite the acquittal, the sentence, confirmed by the Court of Defendants, made it clear that Antonio Gava, as well as local politicians of his party, had links with the Camorra. The court accused Gava of receiving votes in exchange for services rendered by the Camorra. Many witnesses testify to this, including one powerful witness. The people from Naples, when the Ministry of the Interior passed from Antonio Gava to Vincenzo Scotti, the Neapolitan teasing, "You have heard Mich., the Interior, have gone from D'Alessandro to Nuvoletta."[1]

D'Alessandro e Nuvoletta are both Camorra's clan leaders linked in business with politicians: the first one (D'Alessandro) with Antonio Gava, and the second one with Vincenzo Scotti.

The famous Camorra rat Pasquale Galasso, whose testimony led to the arrest of dozens of people, several times mentioned the name of Antonio Gava as an acquaintance of clan leaders. Moreover, how could the viceroy Gava have won tens of thousands of votes, for himself and other politicians, without the consent of the Camorra? Everyone knows that the Camorra controls the votes, because in Naples, the population of Camorra is estimated to be 300 thousand, not counting the people who live with them. Some newspapers wrote that the Camorra in Naples does not exist. It 'Naples, the Camorra itself

As a conclusion to this strange case, the grandson of Gava, on behalf of his deceased uncle, demanded 40 million Euros from the state as compensation for the injustices suffered in the previous thirteen years.

Note:

I would bet 100,000 euro against the grandson of Antonio Gava, and remake the process to his grandfather, but not in Italy. We take the dossier of the process and we go to Austria, Germany, Switzerland, England, Holland, Sweden, Norway, England, Iceland and USA and Australia. He will have an embarrassment of choice, but one thing is certain, in any court of these countries were judged, he will certainly be condemned, and this I assure you.

The things that happen in Italy are unlikely to happen in those countries.

With all the evidence accusations against Antonio Gava, it is surprising that the grandson asks damages arguing the innocence of his grandfather. In the Italian courts, due process exists only for the poor.

Paolo Cirino Pomicino
Born Napoli, 1939
Campania region
Graduated in Medicine and Surgery

1 time Minister for the Budget and Economic Planning
1 time Minister of Public

Pomicino began his political career with the Christian Democrats, where he was elected deputy in 1976. He continued over the years to be elected by the DC, until 1994, when this party fell. In 2004 he was elected as a deputy in the party of Clemente Mastella. In 2010, adheres to 'UDC political party of Gianfranco Rotondi.

In the past, during the process for Enimont bribes he was sentenced to 20 months imprisonment. He was also implicated in the Irpinia earthquake scandal, where he was involved in the mismanagement of funds. This offense, as happens in Italy for most politicians, fell into prescription

Vincenzo Scotti
Born Napoli, 1933
Campania region
Degree in law
1-time Minister of Labour and Social Security
1-time Minister of Cultural Heritage and Activities
1-time Minister of Civil Protection
1-time Minister of the Interior
1-time Minister of Foreign Affairs
1-time Undersecretary of the Ministry of Foreign Affairs

The political career of this character starts back in 1968, with the Christian Democrats. And like the others, he disappeared for a while in 1992 with the "Tangentopoli" scandal, laying low until the waters calmed down. He reappeared and politics in 2008, when he was appointed, rather than elected, the undersecretary of state and the ministry of foreign affairs. In 2010, unable to get enough votes to be elected, he founded the "We the south" party, becoming its president.

He has been convicted of embezzling funds from the SISDE. Offense prescribed but despite this, the Court of Accounts of the Government has obliged him to return about 3 million Euros.

Italian Communist Party

The Communist Party of Italy was born in 1921 in Livorno (Tuscany) from the splitting of a part of politicians belonging to the Italian Socialist Party. It was only in 1943 that became known as the Italian Communist Party.

Since 1947, the Italian Communist Party is the second largest party elected in Italy. Since the early years, its leader, Togliatti, has emulated the Communists in Moscow. After the death of Togliatti in 1964, the leadership fell to Luigi Longo, who had been deputy secretary of the party since its foundation.

We should remember his opposition to the invasion of Czechoslovakia by the Soviet Union, which took place in 1968. That year, Longo supports the Secretary of the Communist Party of Czechoslovakia, Alexander Dubcek, who wanted to break away from Moscow to make his country a free socialist state, as opposed to the Soviet one, which took away the freedoms of people. This began to mark the difference in culture between Soviet Communism and Italian Communism, the latter of which was accustomed to individual liberty and freedom for its people, neither of which existed in the Soviet Union. In 1969, as the assistant secretary of Luigi Longo, Berlinguer had a speech that scandalized all the other Communist leaders of the world, who were present at the international congress in Moscow. He called the invasion of Czechoslovakia an unjust attack against free people. This was the beginning of the

Italian Communist Party's break with Moscow, which was understood to be too unreasonable and oppressive.

In 1972 Longo resigned as secretary of the party. He was replaced by Enrico Berlinguer (for me, the greatest character in the PCI). In the mid-70s, Berlinguer made a speech in Moscow, during the International Communist Congress on, before thousands of delegates, saying that in Italy you could build a socialist society that was equitable and just, and that this was his desire. This way of thinking led Berlinguer and his party to a slight win over the Christian Democrats in the 1976 elections.

At this time, Berlinguer tried, with his famous "historic compromise", to get his party into the country's government with the Christian Democrats. In fact, in 1978 they had already been in contact with Aldo Moro (Secretary of the DC), who on 16 March of that year was kidnapped by the Red Brigades. On 9 May of that year, Aldo Moro was killed. With his death, the possibility of creating a socialist society in Italy died also. It is my conviction that Italy with Berlinguer would have created a socialist society better than the current Chinese one. Berlinguer had deep respect for the people; always looking out for their interests and allowing people and businesses to be free. This was Mr. Berlinguer, a true gentleman.

Berlinguer will remain forever in the memory of the Italians for his fight against corruption in politics. He was only the second character, after Giorgio Almirante (leader of the Italian Social Movement—MSI) to expose corruption in politics, his flagship cause.

No one knows who arranged the death of Aldo Moro, whether it was the CIA or Italian terrorists financed by Russia. But one thing is certain: someone did not want the "historic compromise" between the Christian Democrats and the Communists.

In 1984, during a rally in Padua, Berlinguer had a stroke. He tried to finish his speech but went into a coma at the hotel and was taken to hospital, where he died shortly after. His funeral was celebrated in Rome, and 1 million people attended. Even his political rivals, including Giorgio Almirante, went to pay their respects. He was one of the few Italian politicians that most of the people loved. He was replaced by Party Secretary Alessandro Natta.

In 1989, Achille Occhetto took the place of of Natta, and during the same year, after the fall of the Berlin Wall, differences began to rise within the Communist Party. In 1991, at the Congress of the Delegates in Rimini, the party was dissolved. Out of this schism two parties were worn: the Democratic Left Party (PDS), with 67 per cent of the vote, and the Refounded Communist Party of PRC with 33 per cent. In 1994 after the resignation of Achille Occhetto as secretary of the PDS, Massimo D'Alema took his place. In 1995 the PDS entered the centre-left Olive Coalition, led by Romano Prodi. Prodi won the election in 1996 and for the first time the PDS would be part of the Italian government.

In 1998, under the guidance of Massimo D'Alema, a new political entity was born, comprised of PDS and politicians from other political parties. The PDS became the Democratic Left (DS). To this day it is the party that wins the second most votes in Italy. Its leader is Pierluigi Bersani.

Italian Socialist Party

The Italian socialist party was born in Genoa in 1892 as the Italian Workers' Party, founded by Filippo Turati and other people. In the 1910 Congress in Milan, differences began to emerge giving rise to two movements.

The party underwent a great metamorphosis, with continuous changes in name and split forming other parties. Many people in this party would go on to found other parties from 1910 onwards Even after the war, in 1950 there were discrepancies between the different souls of socialism, in fact, many exiles founded the Italian Democratic Socialist Party, a party close to the left wing, while the Italian Socialist Party was part of the government with the Christian Democrats, a party this last, bitter enemy of the left-wing parties.

In 1978 the party's national Congress, with more than 60 per cent of the vote, elected Secretary Craxi, who, in the same year declared a complete withdrawal from Marxist ideology to promote the liberal ideology of socialism. However, you have to wait until 1985 to see the hammer and sickle completely removed from their political symbol. This was replaced by a red carnation, which would it disappear and 1994 following "Tangentopoli", two years after the beginning of the scandal, in which they were involved, many politicians of the Italian Socialist Party.

The end of 1994 marked the death of the PSI, which had many of its politicians involved in taking bribes, beginning with Craxi. Since the dissolution of the party, several others have arisen. Among them include Berlusconi's centre-right party and Prodi's with coalition of centre-left party

Bettino Craxi
Born in Milano, 1934
Lombardia region
Dead in Hammamet (Tunisia) 2000

1-time Chairman of the Board

It was Craxi who, as chairman of the board, helped Berlusconi's TV stations obtain a license to broadcast over the national territory. On the other hand, Berlusconi funded Craxi's party with tens of billions of lire. The partnership is now in the past, leaving both men more than satisfied. Craxi was the only person to whom the Italian people did so much harm, in the aftermath of the bribery scandal, which began in

February 1992 with the arrest of a member of the Socialist Party Mr. Mario Chiesa, while he was cashing a bribe.

Mr Chiesa explained to the magistrates in Milan the system of bribes that he had in place in that city. This scandal was the beginning of a great downgrading of the Italian Socialist Party

When he realized that Milan's magistrates were intending to prosecute mainly politicians of his party, Craxi, on July 3 1992, made the following statement to Members of the parliament: "Who among you has the courage to swear he never resorted to illegal financing for the party? Will you swear in court here? Does any one of you feel so clean?" No one took up the challenge.

In December 1992 Craxi received his first notice to appear in court. Throughout the country there was a great hatred towards this political figure. I too, unfortunately, hated him for what he was accused of. I was ignorant then, and I apologize for my feelings towards him. Craxi was the only political figure who had the courage to tell the truth. This happened about twenty years ago. Unfortunately, the dirty games continue to this day, despite the rules that were put in place. In his last speech, on 29 April 1993, he spoke admirably:

"It time to stop being hypocrites. All parties have taken bribes to finance themselves. Even those in here who are the moralists have taken bribes. I am no worse than you. All of us have taken bribes."

That same day on April 29 1993, despite numerous warrant of arrest actually received from the magistrate of Milano, the Chamber of Deputies refused permission to proceed against him causing the wrath of public opinion and by scandal at several newspapers.

Never was a politician in Italy treated as badly as Craxi. He simply found himself in the wrong place at the wrong time. Had it been anyone else, he would have been treated the same way. Just think of the several thousand people gathered in Piazza Navona to listen to the speeches of the Secretary of the PDS Mr. Achille Occhetto, along with other politicians Rutelli and Ayala:they urged all those present to protest the parliamentary vote in favour of Craxi. However, the immunity that many others received, according to those who protested, was not to be applied to Craxi. So why the politicians do not obliterated this law? A small procession, organized by the northern League, finally pulled up the Pantheon Piazza Colonna. Coinciding with the end of the rally held in Piazza Navona, a mob invaded Largo Febo expecting Craxi to leave the Raphael Hotel, which had been his home for years. When Craxi left the hotel, he was targeted by protesters, who pelted him with objects, especially coins, as well as insults and mocking chants. With the help of police, Craxi was able to climb into the car and left the hotel. This episode, broadcast hundreds of times by TG, is now taken as a symbol of Craxi's political order. He once described it as "a kind of fire" in an interview with Giuliano Ferrara, broadcast on Channel 5.

In May 1994, to avoid arrest, Craxi fled to Hammamet in Tunisia, where he was sure he would not be extradited to Italy. Since then he has lived in Tunisia, and many Italian politicians have gone to see him. From Hammamet, Craxi continued to accuse the judges involved in Operation Clean Hands of not being impartial. He accused them of wanting to hit his party, protecting the PDS.

He died of a heart attack on 19 January 2000, still at large and wanted by the Italian government. There are politicians in Italy who have done much worse damage than he did, even one who is still a senator for life.

This is life, this is Italy—willy-nilly.

Note:

The Craxi's Socialist Party had loans of several billion Lire from Berlusconi, which in my opinion, was the only one able to move a little political power from Rome to Milan. Silvio Berlusconi was probably fed up with always having to go to Rome for some important license. With Craxi as Prime Minister in fact, he was able to organize his television empire in no time. I've always wondered why there was never a Clean Hands pool in the 70s or 80s. How strange, when the power shifted a little in Milan, Italian magistrates became aware of corruption, as if before, there had never been. In my opinion there is in southern Italy Masonic organization, knowing that if the North of the country were to achieve the secession, the South would fail instantly. Currently, the unification of 'Italy is desired only by the politicians of the south, who are colonizing the north transferring large numbers of southern populations in the north in all public areas of the state as policemen, police, army, professors, teachers, managers and all others possible sector, whereas in my country, the Veneto, young people must emigrate.

Chapter 3

Operation Clean Hands

From 1992 to 1994 there were major policy changes in the country. The "Tangents" scandal began with the arrest of a Socialist politician who was pocketing a bribe of 7 million lire. This was followed by a succession of other arrests, sparking a political change in the country. Between those years, thanks to the arrest of several politicians of other political parties, two major Italian parties disappeared: the Christian Democrats and the Socialist Party. In 1993, the Radical Party won a resounding success in a referendum proposed. Over 90 per cent of Italians were in favor of abolishing public financing of political parties.

The parties, nearly all of them having lost funding through illegal kickbacks, and now with the public against public funding, began to study other forms of financing. These included contributions to election expenses and public funds to the media. It is estimated that over the last sixteen years, the policy has cost the citizens €3 billion. In one-way or another the politicians must always collect. It is the Italian style.

The arrest of Mario Chiesa began a great evolutionary process in Italian politics. From 1992 to 1999 more than two thousand politicians were arrested, including representatives of the major Italian parties, from simple politicians to deputies and senators, all involved in this deeply rooted system of bribes.

In their book "La deriva. perchè l'Italia rischia il naufragio"(the drift—because Italy is in danger of sinking), journalists Stella and Rizzo reported that, since the 60s, politicians had become interested in public procurement, These journalists did a thorough investigation, and they discovered that before politicians entered it the public procurement system, the Italian infrastructure (highways, roads, bridges, etc.) had progressed very well—the costs were contained. However, when politicians took control of the contracts, the costs increased significantly. Therefore, in my opinion, Operation Clean Hands broke too late. In thirty years, the economic damage caused by the policy was elevated; indeed, the debt that Italy has today was caused by the politics of the past.

In their search for absolute power and money to finance their campaigns, the major political parties created this monster, contributing to the birth of new generations of politicians and businessmen that became rotten and corrupt (the latter of which soon became accustomed to politicians' continuous requests for money). This increased the cost of the work to build Italy's infrastructure, as businessmen would compete to see who would be offered the highest bribe to win the contract. It is natural that in such a system, many unscrupulous individuals will take advantage for private achieve, without regard for anyone. Few people started the political carrier because of pure passion.

Here is one case in point of the malfeasance committed at the time: Italy started the 1950s well, and in just eight years, from 1956 to 1964, they built the Autostrada del Sole (Highway of the Sun), a length of 755 km with many tunnels and viaducts. The parties were not yet involved in public procurement. The chief engineer of the Highway of the Sun, in 1968, Fedele Cova, was quick to denounce the interference of politicians in the procurement of works, as he saw that politicians wanted to entrust the construction projects to their friends and relatives.

Today, the entire country is paying the price for this political mess. Health is one area, in particular, that is suffering. Daniela Minerva wrote a book discussing this topic, "LA FIERA DELLE SANITA'—politici corrotti. medici ciarlatani-" THE FAIR OF HEALTHCARE—corrupt politicians-medical charlatans. In this book she cited fraud and inefficiency among the major abuses, endangering the health of the Italians. In a serious country, this book would be enough to spark a revolution. In Italy, nothing has happened.

Italy is a country resigned. It is a country defeated by its own people. I firmly believe that the roots of this problem originate in southern Italy, where there is a sense of entitlement to public money among politicians. Sadly, it is a mentality that we in the north are acquiring as well. In southern Italy, the chief of a department acts as the master of that department, not as a subordinate of the department head.

All over the decades, all the parties have propagated this criminal system. Consider the unjust arrest warrant against Craxi; if you wanted real justice, you would have to take legal action to the members of all the parties. People in the 90s scapegoat Craxi, unaware that this system existed before him, that politicians from all parties had been taking bribes for decades.

This is not to mention organized crime's direct impact on public works. I remember my junior high school days when, in parts of the south, the Mafia would blow up pillars of the future viaduct. I remember what I had to say about this at the time: "If they pull down the pillars because they want money, we should just avoid building roads there." I was young then, and this was my analysis.

The road I'm referring to is the Autostrada infinita(the infinite highway): the Salerno-Reggio Calabria. In 1964, construction began on the highway, and despite the difficulties involved—the terrain and the impact of organized crime—it was completed in 1972. It was not as well built as the Highway of the Sun, built previously, as a few years later work still needed to be done to improve it. Today it is still called Autostrada infinita o Autostrada dai mille cantieri(the Infinite Highway or the Highway with a Thousand Yards). I challenge you to find any country in the world that has spent as much money per mile on a highway as the Salerno-Reggio Calabria. When

Minister of Public Works Lunardi (Berlusconi government) said on TV, "Unfortunately, in southern Italy we are forced to live and work with Camorra and 'Ndrangheta organized crime," I was almost a heart attack. How could a minister make such a statement on national TV? Is he suggesting that whoever wins a contract has to pay a bribe to, hire staff from, and buy cement and other materials from organized crime?

If the whole of Italy is going adrift, as journalists Stella and Rizzo say in their book, it is due to criminal organizations in the south. With the help of some writers, I will provide evidence. While it is true that even the politicians of northern Italy did nothing to stop this social cancer, this does not change the fact that if Veneto (my country) were a republic, completely separated politically from Italy, the Venetian people would lead better lives and would not suffer the same fate as Greece. Unfortunately, it looks as though this will be the case. Each country gets what it deserves, it is true.

Operation Clean Hands involved more than two thousand politicians, more than twenty thousand summons to appear before the investigating judge and 9 people killed themselves. There are many more things to say about the events leading up to 1994, during the First Republic, and many more inconceivable events (at least for a normal person) to relate. I do not point the finger at any of the particular parties—left, right, centre, or otherwise—but I merely look at the facts raw and real that occurred before 1994, before the first Berlusconi government.

Chapter 4

The Italian Government from 1992 to 2011

1st Amato	1992-1993

1st Amato   1992-1993

Ciampi   1993-1994

1st Berlusconi   1994-1995

Dini   1995-1996

1st Prodi   1996-1998

1st D'Alema   1998-1999

2nd D'Alema   1999-2000

2nd Amato   2000-2001

2nd Berlusconi   2001-2005

3rd Berlusconi   2005-2006

2nd Prodi   2006-2008

4th Berlusconi   2008-present

From Operation Clean Hands until 2000, there were eight governments in Italy. This was followed by a period of relative stability, with four governments in eleven years.

Table X.X Major Political Parties of the Second Republic to Date

Party	Leader
People of Freedom	Silvio Berlusconi
Democratic Party	Pier Luigi Bersani
Northern League	Umberto Bossi
Christian Democratic Union (Udc)	Pier Ferdinando Cadini
Italy of Values	Antonio Di Pietro
Future and Freedom	Gianfrenco Fini

Note: In addition to these there are thirteen others.

1996-2011: Unfair, Rotten, and Corrupt Government

Prodi government   17 April 1996-21 October 1998
D'Alema government   21 October 1998-25 April 2000
Amato government   25 April 2000-11 June 2001

Political coalition made up of: "Ulivo" (all left parties), and "other independent parties"

Romano Prodi
Born in Scandiano-Reggio Emilia
Graduated in law
Chairman of the Board

Prodi was tied to the Christian Democrats, and from 1983 to 1989 he was the president of the IRI (Institute for Industrial Reconstruction), the Italian public institution founded in 1933 on the initiative of Benito Mussolini to save failing Italian banks. In the 1950s the IRI helped the country's economic development. In the 1980s, Prodi was commissioned by the government to sell the industries owned by IRI, because in those years many companies were operating at a loss. You will review it again in '93 for one year only, as President of IRI, to continue the privatization of government companies. In 1995, Prodi, along with other leftist parties, founded the Olive Coalition, comprising all parties on the left. In 1996 he won the election against Berlusconi, thanks to the coalition he formed with many on the left, including the extreme left. His formula seems to have been "Whoever does not like Berlusconi is welcome to come with me."

Just like Giorgio Napolitano, Prodi, after decades of political experience in Italy, and knowing all its cultures, did nothing to remedy its problems. It's the classic Italian mentality: people are as they are—what can I do? So the propagation of criminal organizations and fraud against the State continued.

Dear Prodi, earlier with the Christian Democrats is another matter, but in 1996 as president of the board, could you not have triggered the moral recovery of the country? Instead of continuing to allow injustices, dear Prodi, you should have done what any reasonable man would do when taking the reins of a country so culturally diverse:

1. Control wasteful public spending, especially in the south. Wage war not only on tax evaders in the north, as you did in 2006, but in all areas of the country. Declare war on criminal organizations.
2. If you are unable to put the south in line, then favor the division of the country into two. It's not fair that the north should have to work to maintain a government complicit in Mafia affairs when the people of the south barely pay any taxes at all.

A recent episode of the program *Report* on RAITRE demonstrates just how politically inept Italy is these days. Tax skirting was among the topics discussed. The German government recently bought a list of German citizens who have bank accounts in Switzerland from an employee of a Swiss bank. With this, the German government was able to recover 1.8 billion Euros in lost tax revenues at a cost of 10 million Euros. In Italy, the Constitutional Court has prohibited the state from doing the same thing because it is illegal. Are we crazy? Thank you, Mr Prodi, for making our country such a bastion of goodness. In a country so corrupt, you must be equally hard, dear Prodi.

Giorgio Napolitano
Born in Napoli
Minister of the Interior

Since 1953, Napolitano has continually been elected to the Italian Communist Party in the district of Naples. Everybody knows that the Camorra controls the votes in the city. What does this say about his record? I think it speaks volumes that as both minister of the interior and president of the republic, he has never once fought against organized crime. Evidently, the problem of the roads in Naples, always clogged with garbage, is not his concern either.

Note:

When I think that the newspaper "The New York Times" had the courage to call this political figure "King George the savior of Italy," makes me think that not only the author of this article was drunk when he wrote that such a hoax but those control officers were more than drunken, drugged perhaps. Define savior of Italy a person who for decades has always been elected in the city of Naples, is an insult to all normal people of this world. Surely millions of Italians will be very offended and I hope that one day the New Yorker newspapier, recognizes the offense caused by such an outrageous article.

Angelo Giorgianni
Born in Reggio Calabria
Undersecretary of the Interior

Giorgianni in '98 was forced by Prime Minister Romano Prodi to resign after allegations of collusion with the Mafia in Messina.

This person who is a magistrate since 1977, and then entered politics, is involved in shady dealings with the mafia, is considered extremely dangerous and should be isolated. However, as always happens in the south, after the bribery scandal, which broke out in city of Messina (Sicily) in 1998, in which Giorgianni, was involved along with many others, the process ended with the acquittal of all defendants.

Giorgianni In 2001 he returned to work as a magistrate.

But how many corrupt people there are all over Italy in the Italian judiciary?

But how many false processes, with the acquittal of criminals occur in Italy every day as one of Giorgianni, which were all acquitted? A society like that makes me very afraid.

ARE ITALIAN GOOD PEOPLE?

In 2001 the centre-left Amato government, passes a law against all Italians.

Such law made it possible for foreigners over 65 of age living in Italy to get 550 Euros a month as a social allowance. This law has done nothing but increase the elderly population in the country. Just think of all foreigners residing in Italy who brought their parents into the country just to receive the 550 Euros a month that the rich Italian government was prepared to give. The absurdity of what was happening was that the immigrant, to let in the elderly parent in Italy, was to ensure the livelihood of the same to the Italian government. Upon entering Italy, the aged father was sent to seek a livelihood to the government agency, and the game was made. Is not that absurd?

Since 2001, hundreds of thousands of foreigners over sixty-five years of age received the social allowance of 550 Euros per month. In the city of Cremona (Lombardy Region), a magistrate (what I call a rare honest employee of the State) commissioned the Guardia di Finanza to see if foreigners who received financial aid by the government were really living in the city. It turns out more than half of the people, had returned to their country of origin: Albania, Morocco and China. What a marvellous law have you made idiots of the left!

In February 1998 during training, an American military plane severed the wires of the cable in Cermis in Val di Fiemme, in the province of Trento. In the cabin, which fell from 80 meters in height were killed 20 persons of different nationalities. Only thanks to the readiness of the magistrate of Trent was able to accuse the American aircraft components, but unfortunately the perpetrators of the massacre were tried in U.S.A. I still remember the justice minister Diliberto, who swapped the two American soldiers with the release of Silvia Baraldini.

The pilot and his assistant were tried and convicted in the United States, but the minister of defense Diliberto (a communist idealist), managed to secure the return of Silvia Baraldini, who was serving a forty-three-year sentence in the United States for subversive association, escape from prison, two attempted robberies, and contempt of court. In 1999, Justice Minister Oliviero Diliberto, he went to Rome airport to receive this companion Communist Silvia Baraldini, as it were a head of state, and accompanied her in the Roman prison of Rebibbia. In 2001 she was placed under house arrest, and in 2006 was given a grace.

The Prodi's center-left coalition, lost the election in 2001, because of their absurd behavior towards the Italian people. Just consider the allocation of housing, or have benefits in municipal kindergartens, well, foreigners were increasingly advantaged in obtaining these services, while the Italians had to turn to the private market, far more expensive. Unfortunately the facts are real, sometimes leading to a racism towards the stranger. And I can not forget the reaction of citizens of the city of Modena in the post office, who were angry at the sight of foreigners, to collect a larger pension. And see that some foreigners could not even make themselves understood, we can imagine the reaction, may have had, a pensioner who after 40 years of work receives 525 Euros a month pension, while the alien receives 550, having never worked in Italy. People, think well what injustice must suffer the elderly in Italy.

Silvio Berlusconi
Born in Milan
Chairman of the Board
2nd Berlusconi government
3rd Berlusconi government

Political coalition of Forza Italia, National Alliance(Alleanza Nazionale), the Northern League(Lega Nord) and four other minor parties

I think that Silvio Berlusconi is the most investigated of the political world, with more than 20 processes, some ongoing, others prescribed, and others already concluded by determining his innocence.

An ordinary citizen would already be in prison. One thing is certain: with regard to politics, if it were not him, whom else? There are too many politics in Italy, which have always created mystification and instability.

Berlusconi was the one who promoted the law decriminalizing "false accounting". I cannot imagine a more infamous law. Who would willingly pay taxes when such laws invite you to evade them? (However, in 2006, when the Prodi government won the election, why did they not erase this disgraceful law?)

While it is a fact that during his tenure he made many laws to safeguard himself from the judiciary, without him, who is good enough to take his place?

The problem with Berlusconi, in my opinion, is that he thought too much for himself and two little for his country. He has demonstrated himself to be a very capable public figure; he is just too self-seeking.

Giuseppe Pisanu
Born in Ittiri
Minister of the Program

In the early 80s Pisanu was forced to resign from the post of Undersecretary of the Treasury due to his association with the Masonic Lodge P2, in particular with Roberto Calvi and Flavio Carboni, who were responsible for the failure of the Banco Ambrosiano, of which Calvi was the president.

Claudio Scaiola
Born In Imperia
Minister of the Program

Scaiola became famous in Italy in the corruption scandal for helping an entrepreneur obtain contracts from Civil Defense. In fact, he turned out to be the person whom a mysterious individual had bought an apartment for near the Coliseum.

Note:

This politician was the youngest (34 years) mayor of Italy in the city of Imperia. His father was the founder of the Christian Democratic political party in the city of Imperia in Liguria region. He was repeatedly accused of corruption and was always acquitted.

And again I repeat that the Italian justice system is at the level of the fourth world; in the third world it works better.

2nd Prodi Government, 17 April 2006-6 April 2008
Political Centre-Left Coalition Made Up of Twenty-Two Parties

This government, nicknamed the "armed Brancaleone", lasted two years, the time required to apply a minimum tax severity. The problem was that such strictness as applied only in northern Italy. While it is true that it helped the government increase tax revenues by 11 billion Euros, all it does is pay down the debt incurred by the regions of the south. As always, the north is plundered to save the south from debt.

In 2006 this government approved a pardon that, in August, saw more than 22,000 released from prison, gradually building up to 27,000 people by January 2007. It is estimated that in three years' time, 30 per cent of inmates returned to prison because they committed new crimes. Rather than pardon these detainees they should have built prison-factories so these inmates could be a resource and not a cost for the country.

Massimo D'Alema
Born in Roma
Vice Chairman of the Board

It is very famous his sentence against the pool of "clean hands" calling <Soviets in Milan>, since the magistrates in Milan began to investigate the bribery of the then Italian Communist Party, to which he belonged.

For years he rented a state-owned apartment in Rome, paying rent much lower than market value (*affittopoli* scandal).

Francesco Rutelli
Born in Roma
Vice Chairman of the Board

When he was mayor of Rome (for eight years, as the head of the centre-left coalition), he was sentenced by the court to indemnify the municipality of Rome (he paid 40.000 Euros), for it led to "external expertise" when the town had the same personal service qualified for such advice.

Note:

THIS IS THE TYPICAL CHEATING IN A VERY ITALIAN STYLE, UNFORTUNATELY.

Alfonso Pegoraro Scanio
Born in Salerno

As Environment Minister, a role in which he was utterly incompetent, he was known as the "Mr No"—no to incinerators because they pollute, no to wind turbines because they spoil the environment, no this and no to that. When he reached the end of his tenure as Environment Minister, Naples was floating in trash. It is obvious that he always had the best interests of the oil industry in mind.

Note:

This idiot and infamous was environment minister of the Prodi's government for two years from 2006 to 2008. Even you Mr. Pegoraro such as your countryman and President of the Republic Giorgio Napolitano are an incompetent and uncaring. But what we wanted to build some incinerators as there is in northern Italy? Were you afraid of the Camorra, perhaps? Or you felt proud to see the city of Naples with tons of garbage that occupied entire streets?

You of the South, you are lazy and good for nothing.

4ᵗʰ Berlusconi government 8 May 2008-present
Political coalition of Popolo delle libertà and Lega Nord
Giuseppe Ciarrapico
Born in Roma
Businessman

This political figure, with huge problems with the law follows Berlusconi very well. In fact, in the mid-70s he was sentenced by the magistrate to pay a fine for using child labour, a ruling the Supreme Court affirmed. He was sentenced in the Supreme Court to three years in prison for a crash in bankruptcy of 70 billion lire. He was sentenced along with his son Tullio, and others, in the Italsanita accounting scandal in 1993. After being released from prison, he was then sentenced by the court of Milan for illegal financing of political parties. In 2000 he was convicted in the Supreme Court, but because of his "advanced age" (that being sixty-six years old), he was assigned to social services.

He was sentenced in 1998 to four years and six months in prison for his part in the collapse of Banco Ambrosiano (whose president was Roberto Calvi). At that time, thanks to two amnesties, he found himself having to serve a six-month sentence. He was pardoned for the remaining four years, and he served the remaining six months of his sentence under house arrest because of ill health.

In 2011 the Court of Accounts asked Ciarrapico to return 45 million Euros, obtained illegally as a government grant to the press, therefore defrauding the state.

In the 2008 elections he was elected senator in Berlusconi's People of Freedom.

Note:

This character is another classic example of how justice functions in Italy, where the crooks rule over the people and the poor are sent to prison for petty theft.

Nicola Cosentino
Born in Casal di Principe-Caserta
Degree in Law

Cosentino began his political career in the late 70s, holding various positions in his place of birth. At the national level he began his with the Forza Italia party, and is elliptical in '96 as a deputy, a position he regained in the elections of 2001 and 2006. In the 2008 general election he joined the government as secretary of state's economy and finances.

In 2008 he had already been implicated in a scandal involving the recycling of toxic waste, but it would take a year of investigations before the judiciary issued a notice of detention for the offense of external association with the Camorra. An arrest warrant was presented to the House of Representatives, but they refused to execute it. The court of Naples also prohibited the use of evidence in a wiretapping indictment.

Following his resignation from the government as secretary in July 2010, he became the secretary of the PDL in Campania, a position he holds to this day.

Cosentino was a frequent topic in the national news; in fact, the majority asked him to resign because of this.

It should also be emphasized that Cosentino's brother-in-law is a boss of the Camorra.

In the summer of the same year, there was approval of the Lodo Alfano, who is in the law, there is the suspension of criminal trials for the 4 highest offices of state: President of the Republic, Chairman of the Board, President the room and the president of the senate. In a little over 1 month, the Lodo Alfano (known as saving processes, for Berlusconi) was approved.

Unfortunately, in the centre-left many are hungry for power, and it is difficult to satisfy everyone. This is the Italian problem: too many parties. The problem would be solved if a maximum of three parties were allowed to run. Then, left-wing politics, more and more favourable to immigrants and criminals, has shifted the votes in the centre right, to Berlusconi.

Unfortunately this was a useless gesture, as the left has forgotten its own people. This is the fortune of Berlusconi.

In January 2010, try to approved the law is the "short process", which shortens the process and then you arrive earlier, prescription. Berlusconi saved his butt. Again, this was thanks to the stupidity and incapability of the left (or at least most members of it). Fortunately, they failed to pass this infamous law. The 'short process' law favoured delinquents and criminals, in coming free from prosecution. Fortunately, in June 2011, the Council of Europe, groom Italy, for too much corruption, and the law that the Italian government wanted to approve. Indeed, this law has not yet been approved.

It is needless to go on listing examples of corruption in the Berlusconi government. Suffice it to say this is the social disaster we have been handed down by the Christian Democrats of the 1960s, so what can we expect now? Unfortunately, to win elections both the centre-left and the centre-right must rely on votes handed to them by the underworld, culled from high density southern regions. I'm speaking of Campania, Sicily, which alone has 11 million inhabitants, not to mention other Mafia regions, such as Calabria and Puglia, which contained another 6 million. (This is out of the total national population of 60 million people.) You can then add to this the corrupt regions of Rome and Lazio. There are too many regions in Italy in which politicians must rely on underworld support to get elected. And while it is true that not all people are corrupt, unfortunately, the Mafia in the south are now powerful enough that they possess an enormous amount of political capital.

For many decades they have continued splurging without anyone saying anything. On 6 November 2011, on the TV program *Report* Milena Gabanelli explained how banks have been evading hundreds of millions of Euros in taxes. How old are the systems that they are exploiting to avoid paying these taxes?. And who owns the shares of these banks, whic should be paying taxes on capital gains to the state? After what you have told Gabanelli, as you are sure that the bank pays the taxes of others, to the state? Let's be realistic. "REPORT" on Raitre, is the only instructive program that does not look at anybody.

Think of the absurdity of the Italian Constitutional Court, which forbade the Italian government from acquiring the names of Italian citizens who had money in Switzerland. It is impracticable to understand the madness of this court and the crimes they have permitted these dodgers to commit against the Italian people.

Regardless, none of this corruption has anything to do with the culture of the North, which has developed as the South has lagged behind.

From FORZA ITALIA(FORC ITALY) in 1994

To POPOLO DELLE LIBERTA'(PEOPLE OF FREEDOM) in 2008

Silvio Berlusconi
Born in Milan, 1936
Leader
4-time Chairman of the Board

This gentleman could very well enter the *Guinness Book of World Records* as the most investigated politician in the world.

Berlusconi is responsible for financing and otherwise assisting the Italian Socialist Party of Craxi. The evidence of such support is now proven. However, one must remember that Berlusconi does not do a thing for nothing. In all these activities, there was a simple agenda: to shift the political power (and therefore decision-making) from Rome to Milan. Without this, Berlusconi could never have created the television empire we know today. It is the Italian culture that made this political direction possible, by allowing corruption and tax evasion to go unchecked. It in a country like Finland, it never would have happened. Over there he never would have had a chance to bribe his way to power. He is the son of a rotten and corrupt political system that began in the 50s and continues to this day.

Of course, those on the left will absolve themselves of guilt, playing the role of the innocent saint. But it must be noted that in postwar Italy, almost all the parties helped build the rotten, corrupt system we have today.

Berlusconi began his entrepreneurial career in the building industry, building Milano 2 and other organizations. However, when challenged, he could not answer how he generated the capital that allowed him to begin his great career as an entrepreneur. More than once, Berlusconi availed himself of the right to remain silent, before the magistrate, as to the origin of large sums of money, which he used to fund his companies. This is now proven, particularly after Swiss law changed to reveal the holders of certain monies. Banca Rasini has been implicated in laundering money for gangsters. In addition to Silvio Berlusconi, their customers included Sicilian Mafia bosses Bernardo Provenzano and Toto Riina. In addition, Berlusconi's fortune is tied to his father Louis, Banca Rasini's attorney, who made it easy for his son to borrow money.

For fifteen years Berlusconi ran his construction operation. Then, in 1978, he founded Milan Fininvest, a holding company. From 1970 to 1984 he bought three private television stations, which eventually led to the founding of Mediaset. He also founded other building companies, as well as companies in other industries. His most important companies during this period were Publitalia 80, the advertising arm of his television operations, and Reteitalia, which produced and acquired telefilms.

During that time his TV stations began broadcasting nationally. Then, in 1984, magistrates from three cities began blocking transmissions within their territory, because the law forbade private TV stations to broadcast programs across the country. Soon, Berlusconi's friend, Bettino Craxi, as chairman of the board, pushed through a decree in parliament so that Mediaset could continue to broadcast all over the country. Then, in 1990, with the Mammi law (named after Postmaster General Oscar Mammi), we regularized the illegal position of Mediaset, despite many complaints from influential politicians.

Mr Berlusconi would go on to develop interests in TV, insurance, banks, supermarkets, etc.

Then, in 1992, with the "Tangentopoli" scandal, the magistrates of Milan issued weekly arrest warrants against socialist politicians (most recently in early 1994 against Craxi, who in May took refuge in Hammamet in Tunisia to avoid possible arrest).

In March 1994, with his party, Forza Italy, Berlusconi won the elections in alliance with Umberto Bossi's Northern League and Gianfranco Fini's MSI. But in December of that year, the Northern League withdrew from the government, forcing Berlusconi to resign. In 1996, the alliance of centre-left Prodi defeated Berlusconi, who would go on to win the election five years later, in 2001.

In 2006, a grand coalition (Brancaleone Army) led by Prodi defeated Berlusconi by a few thousand votes. In the Senate, Berlusconi had 475,000 more votes in Italy, yet the votes of Italians abroad swung the election toward Prodi. In essence, Italians living abroad decided who was to run Italy. How absurd that the Berlusconi government would allow Italians living abroad to vote and decide the fate of the country.

In January 2008, Minister of Justice Clemente Mastella resigned and the government fell. Mastella brought down the government because the Prodi government was unsympathetic to his wife, who was named in an arrest warrant issued by the prosecutor of Santa Maria Capua Vetere.

On 27 February 2008, Force Italy and Berlusconi and Fini's National Alliance merged to form the People of Freedom(Popolo delle Libertà). In April 2008 the coalition won by an overwhelming margin, in both the House and the Senate. Berlusconi is still president of the board.

I hesitate to list all the charges for which Berlusconi must answer, for there are too many. Here are a few:

- Corruption
- False financial statements
- Illegal financing of political parties
- Tax fraud, tax evasion, and other tax offenses
- False accounting
- Embezzlement

Berlusconi did succeed in decriminalizing false accounting, a terrible crime in my opinion, and one that he is guilty of in most of his businesses. This is unthinkable in a civilized country. What saddens me is that no politician on the left, when get the power, did anything to erase this abominable law. This is an insult to the civil and private area, since tax funds have been pending from both.

Note:

What can I say about Silvio? It 'a nice womanizer, who knows how to communicate with people, and indeed, without him, who pulled out, the devastated Italy? The left incapacitated, who would have further depleted the country? One thing is for sure, Berlusconi in other countries would never have committed any crimes in the past as in Italy, because he would not be allowed. It 'true that in his government, there were many political criminals, that does not mean that there were even 30 years ago, so, please, we know all about Berlusconi because the judiciary and the left-wing newspapers attacked him in all possible ways.

Maybe that's why he bought the sympathy of the people, and even mine sometimes, because a politician, you must attack politically, not because he loves women too much, or because he attended the prostitutes, do not you think?

Cesare Previti
Born Reggio, Calabria, 1934
Lawyer
1-time Minister of Defence

This gentleman is one of the most brazen political figures of the Second Republic. Since the end of the 1970s he has worked for Berlusconi's Fininvest, which over the years has earned him several prosecutions, together with his employer, Berlusconi. In the largest trial (IMI-SIR, in 2006), Previti was sentenced to six years in prison as well as a lifetime ban from public office. This was after he, along with another lawyer, bribed a judge of Rome to decide in favour of Berlusconi on a case. Thanks to a law made the by Berlusconi government for his individual case, Cesare Previti did not serve his penalty. Following this conviction, Previti offered his resignation as deputy.

Note:

Previti is an obnoxious and arrogant character. If the processes were carried out in Italy occurred in the United States, he would be in jail and rot to death, I will assure you.

Marcello Dell'Utri
Born Palermo, 1941
Degree in Law

Here is another character who could never have flourished in a civilized country. He has been involved in so many scandals we can only briefly sum up the most important ones here.

Dell'Utri met Berlusconi during his time studying law in the land. He became a senior officer at Fininvest and one of Berlusconi's trusted friends, founding Forza Italia along with Berlusconi in 1993. In 1995 he was arrested by magistrates in Turin on a charge of making false invoices at Publitalia 80. In 1996 he was elected a deputy in the Berlusconi government, and in 2001 he was elected senator in Forza Italia.

In 1998, in Turin, he was sentenced to three years and two months for tax fraud and creating false spending bills for the company Publitalia. Before the ruling was finalized, Parliament (led by the majority Olive party), hastily passed a law that permitted plea bargains in the Supreme Court. Dell'Utri used it, reducing his sentence to two years and six months, which put him under the three-year threshold requiring one to serve time in prison. His five-year disqualification from public office would remain, however. By virtue of this he lost his seat in Parliament. In the meantime the courts of Palermo had requested his arrest for perjury.

When in 1989 the Italian government passed an amnesty for crimes, not exceeding 4 years of condemnation, Dell'Utri had the courage to apply for amnesty, although he had higher sentences.

The Court of Appeal of Turin rejected the request; however, the Supreme Court accepted it, meaning no additional arrests or penalties.

Note such differences in interpretation of the Amnesty Act of 1989 that there was between the Court of Appeal of Turin and the Supreme Court. It seems that each judge interprets the law to your liking.

Again, the penalty was set at one year and eight months (below the threshold of two years,), after the centre-left Amato government with a new law decriminalized certain financial offenses.

From Milan, meanwhile, came other small penalties for false invoices and false accounting. These were considered a continuation of the charges set in Turin. In 2001 the new Berlusconi government, made a law to further decriminalize the offense of false accounting, which definitely helped Dell'Utri to resolve his legal problems. Meanwhile in Palermo (Sicily) there are two processes for mafia, against Dell'Utri. In the first trial, there is overwhelming evidence that prove collusion between Dell'Utri and the Mafia organization "Cosa Nostra". The Berlusconi's government passed a law that will prohibit the use of wiretaps in judicial proceedings against deputies and senators of the state. Another aid to the deputy Dell'Utri. Despite all these legal problems the deputy Dell'Utri in 2001 was elected senator by taking as many votes in a valuable districts of central Milan.

Marcello confessed on television, "I am applying for self-defence."

Dell'Utri has posed as a man of culture. For example, on 20 June 2003, he inaugurated the library of the Senate palace, in the presence of the President of the Senate, Marcello Pera, and the head of state, Carlo Azeglio Ciampi.

In December 2004, after thirteen days of deliberation, judges of the Second Criminal Chamber of the Court of Palermo sentenced Dell'Utri sentenced to nine years for "criminal association" with the Mafia. The Forza Italia senator was also sentenced to two years probation and was banned from holding public office, in addition to damages awarded in civil suits to the parties, the city, and the province of Palermo. The ruling was read by the President of Guarnotta College, Leonardo, in a room super secure of the Pagliarelli prison in Palermo. Antonio Ingroia and Domenico Gozzo had requested a sentence of eleven years. Seven years was sentenced the mafia boss codefendant Gaetano Cina. A court case began in 1994, after the senator was named a suspect.

I have to say thank you to the website Pummarulella for giving anyone the permission to summarize the anecdote of Dell 'Utri's offenses.

However Dell'Utri is the one who place the Mafia Mr. Mangano, as protector of the Berlusconi family in the 70s, because in those years, the custom of kidnapping had been imported from the South. Mr. Mangano used to live in the Berlusconi's as a groom; that was just a fake role, as Dell'Utri was the one who was ultimately convicted for association with the Mafia.

Note:

In 2007, the senator accumulated more than 40 percent of absences in the Senate, at least if there was a significant fine for each absence, the state would have saved so much money.

Note the territorial origin of all employees and friends of Berlusconi, and their legal problems. And I repeat again that the Italian courts are corrupt beyond belief.

Gianstefano Frigerio
Bachelor of Arts
Born Milano, 1939

Deputy of the Republic by two identities.

Elected in Puglia in Silvio Berlusconi's party, with many posters with the name of Carlo Frigerio a man you can trust.

In Milan, where for Decades in politics is Gianstefano. Yet it is him: as regional secretary of the Christian Democrats in Lombardy (secret and as treasurer of theparty) he received dozens of bribes, was three times arrested between 1992 and 1993, and has-been Involved in many Prosecutions. He has been accused of accepting bribes for landfills Lombard, for a public contract in Monza, in the case of Northern Railway. He admitted to some of the bribes, albeit minimizing his own role in the scandals. For example, he confessed that he had received 150 million Lire from Paolo Berlusconi's Fininvest in exchange for granting the right to manage the landfill in Cerro Maggiore.

He has been convicted for three offenses: 16 months for illegal financing of political parties, 19 months for receiving illicit funds, and 45 months for corruption and bribery. However, after leaving the DC he invented a new life for himself as a personal adviser to and influential member of Silvio Berlusconi's Forza Italia, which directs the research centre. While the judges deliberated on his sentence, Gianstefano would disappear, then reappear, in Puglia as Charles Frigerio, where he earned a seat in Parliament. On 31 May the first meeting day of the new Chamber of Deputies, Frigerio was arrested. He would be sentenced to serve a term of six years and five months. Then he would be assigned to social services, receiving permission to attend Parliament for a few days a month as part of his rehabilitation. (But the judge may not know the rate of deviation of the italian Parliament . . .)

Thanks again to the website Pummarulella for the information they provided on this case.

Note:

This character is the classic characteristics of southern type people, bold and unafraid of anything, as he was not committing anything illegal. And 'true character of this type are known to be friendly to people.

Alfredo Vito
Born Napoli, 1946
Graduated in economics and trade
Deputy of Forza Italia

For those who do not remember, Alfredo Vito, now member of Forza Italia is a former Democrat. He was known by the nickname Il deputato dei centomila voti ("Mr. One Hundred Thousand Preferences"). After confessing to his involvement in the Neapolitan Tangentopoli, he plea-bargained for a two-year sentence and the return of 5 billion lire. Following this he swore, "This marks the end of my political activity."

Note:

Mr. Vito had six judicial proceedings relating to offenses against public administration, however, the prosecution and defence agreed not to proceed. Another proof of the power of money and honesty that there is in Naples. Then offers willingly, 5 billion lire to the City of Naples, who accepts them for intervention in social work? But no judge of Naples had the courage to ask Mr. Vito the provenance of this figure (today's 2.5 million Euros) consistent?

Micciché Gianfranco
Born Palermo, 1954
Manager

Deputy Minister of the Economy, strongman of Forza Italia in Sicily. Several times he has been implicated in relationships with individuals in the Cosa Nostra. Boss Mario Fecarotta, arrested Riina because he nominated him thirty-eight times in two months during telephone conversation, asking him for help with a contract. Micciche was also involved in an ugly story involving cocaine. A Sicilian drug dealer once visited him right in the ministry. Perhaps that is why in Sicily he is spoken of as "one who has his nose." which means "one who sniffs cocaine" (Source: Pummarulella website).

Thanks to his acquaintance with Marcello Dell'Utri (both from Palermo), he became manager of Publitalia 80's Palermo office. In 1994 he was elected a deputy in Forza Italia and became Secretary of the Ministry of Transport.

In 2001 he became Deputy Minister in the Ministry of Economy and Finance. In 2006, Forza Italia was re-elected in great numbers, but he waived his position as deputy to become president of the Sicilian region. He was re-elected in 2008, obtaining the post of Undersecretary of State for the President of the Council. In October 2010, he founded the party Forza Sud to oppose Bossi's Northern League.

Note:

In the world we hear a lot of corruption there is in Italy, forgetting, that most Italian politicians comes from the Deep South. I hope that the evidence presented in this book, do not lead to absurd phrases as is a racist book or anything else. The unequivocal evidence speaks for them.

Nitto Palma
Born Roma, 1950
Magistrate
Minister of Justice since April 2011

Deputy of the Republic. Sicilian lawyer. Leader of Forza Italia. Nino Giuffre, the last of the Mafia "repentant", has mentioned him as having relations with the Cosa Nostra.

Mr. Palma said in an interview that: "The sinking of the Mafia would be useful, but it would be useful to sink even those who oppose to the Mafia."

In 2001 as a deputy proposed a law that would have imposed the suspension of trials for all parliamentarians, to the end of mandate and retroactively. In practice, the full restoration of parliamentary immunity, with the effect of saving their processes both Berlusconi and Dell'Utri is—of course—Cesare Previti.

Note:

From data of 2011 as a senator has been absent for 85 percent of the time

Gaspare Giudice
Born Canicattì, Sicily, 1943
Died Palermo, 2009
Bank Manager

Giudice was acquitted of all the crimes he has been accused of: Mafia association, money laundering, and bankruptcy The offense of criminal association with Costra Nostra is "prescribed" for deadline. See the Italian law on "PRESCRIPTION", which I have already explained.

Deputy of the Republic. Elected in Sicily with Forza Italia. In 1998 mr. Giudice after his arrest, accuses the prosecutor of having made an order of the mafia just to neutralize him as a politician in Sicily. Even Berlusconi said that it is unthinkable that Mr Giudice who is the vice-coordinator of Forza Italy in Sicily, has a connection or business of any kind with the Cosa Nostra, the more so that the deputy Gianfranco Micciche vouched for Mr. Giudice.

According to the indictment, Giudice was in the direct service of Caccamo's Mafia gang, whose men prided them on being elected. There was even a wiretap came to the Chamber of Deputies, in which the mafia reminded to Giudice, do not forget, those who have made him the votes needed to become a deputy. The evidence gathered by the prosecution included the parliamentary authorization to come forward that there was at first persecution against the Parliament.

Even the *supergarantista* Filippo Mancuso had no objections for the prosecutor's request. Yet the Chamber of Deputies on 16 July 1998 vetoed the request for the arrest (by a vote of 303 to 210, with 13 abstentions). Not only that, but deputies were prevented from submitting telecommunications evidence to the court (by a vote of 287 to 239, with 3 abstentions) documenting the relationship and the dependence of Mr. Giudice, from criminal organizations. (Source: Pummarulella website.)

Aldo Brancher
Born Trichiana, 1943
Prete, manager, deputy
1-time Undersecretary to the Department for Institutional Reform
1-time Minister for Subsidiarity and Decentralization

As a young man, Brancher was a priest in the congregation of St. Paul in Alba in the province of Cuneo. In the early 80s he gave up his gown to become a manager in Fininvest. To Berlusconi's company he brought his experience in advertising, and he also wrote for Italy's most popular Catholic weekly magazine "Famiglia Cristiana". In 1993, he was arrested for paying a bribe (as manager of Publitalia 80) of 300 million Lire to the Minister of Health Mr. De Lorenzo, in order to obtain the advertising contract "against 'AIDS" in favor of Fininvest, a Berlusconi's company.

He was arrested and spent three months in prison in San Vittore in Milan, before the terms of custody expired and he was released.

From 1992 to 1994 several hundred people were arrested. The fact that Milan's prosecutor's office could not handle all these cases was to the great fortune of many, including Brancher. Despite the fact that he was convicted of all his offenses (false accounting, illegally financing political parties) he was acquitted after a few years thanks to decriminalization policies (the law made by the Berlusconi government that decriminalized false accounting).

In 2001 he was elected in Veneto with Forza Italia. He continued his political career with Berlusconi, first with Forza Italia then with the People of Freedom, holding positions in different institutions until 2010. Afterworth he was prosecuted and sentenced for the crime of taking over the Antonveneta bank. He was also convicted in the Court of Cassation in 2011, but this charge was dropped think to a pardon granted by the Prodi government in 2006.

On 5 July 2010, due to his association with, Antonveneta, he was forced to resign as Minister for Subsidiarity and Decentralization.

Note:

He discovered this character. He has revealed what it really is, while thousands of clerics still hide inside their clothes. Just consider the case of Cardinal Michele Giordano of Naples, who was involved with his brother for crimes of usury. During the investigation, they found checks issued by the Curia of Naples in the house of a usurer, who was the brother of the Cardinal. Still happen in the Deep South.

Salvatore Sciascia
Born Moglia, Lombardia, 1943
Director of Fininvest tax offices

This former officer of Guardia di Finanza became tax director of Fininvest. It is not difficult to imagine how this position turned out: he was sentenced by the Supreme Court to two years and six months for bribing financiers. He is currently a Senator in the Belusconi's People of Freedom party.

Note:

Here is a great way to get ahead in society. From simple officer of finance at corrupting Director, and finally, Senator of the Italian republic.

It 'true that Berlusconi, led many corrupt people in his government, but we must not forget that he adapted to the Italian system, improving it in order to corrupt and manage the power, causing more damage to the country.

Raffaele Fitto
Born Maglie, Puglia

In October 2009 The prosecutor of Bari indicated Mr. Fitto on charges of criminal conspiracy, corruption, embezzlement, and illegal financing of the party. The process is still going on

In March 2009, the colleague and friend of the same political party then Justice Minister Angelino Alfano, at the Fitto request, sent in Apulia technicians from the Ministry of Justice to investigate against the prosecutors of Bari.

Note:

Note the courage and the guts of the deputy Fitto and the Minister Alfano. Both aware of the veracity of the allegations, believe me.

Chapter 5

Infamous Laws Made by the Berlusconi Government

This chapter details the various infamous laws implemented by the Berlusconi government over the years.

Biondi Decree (1994)

Approved 13 July 1994, by the Berlusconi government, this law prohibits imprisonment for offenses against public administration and financial markets, including corruption and bribery. This law came just as some officers of the Guardia di Finanza confessed to committing acts of corruption for four companies in the Fininvest group (Mediolanum Videotime, Mondadori, and Tele +) and are prepared arrest warrants for managers who paid the bribes.

The decree prevented prosecutors from arresting perpetrators and led to the immediate release of 2764 prisoners, 350 of which were involved in the white-collar Tangentopoli scandal (including Mrs. Maria Di Pierr Poggiolini convicted of bribery with her husband, and former Minister Francesco De Lorenzo and Mr. Antonino Cinà the doctor of mafia boss Toto Riina). People were disgusted to see that criminals like De Lorenzo and Mrs. Poggiolini out of jail, because these two people stole billions Lire causing enormous damage to the Italian state. They cashed in conspicuous bribes from drug companies so that they could increase the final sale price of drugs to the state, or they could market a new drug without waiting for the due time. The protests against the "Salvaladri" (thieves-save) lead parties allied to Berlusconi, Northern League and the National Alliance to withdraw the consent decree and force Berlusconi to let decay in Parliament, because unconstitutional. Soon after they are arrested Paolo Berlusconi, the chief financial officer of Fininvest, Salvatore Sciascia and the consultant group Massimo Maria Berruti.

Note:

Please, I'm not kidding. This above is not a joke, you laugh until you want, but it is the pure truth, real, absurd, inconceivable, certainly impractical in any civilized country, but unfortunately it is true. For me, getting to know these things, now I have surrendered to the Italian mafia governments, past and present. The only exit strategy is to escape.

Tremonti Law (1994

Thanks to Tremonti's decree, made in favor to Berlusconi's profit, the tax exemption for the net enterprise's turnover allow him to earn billions of Lire. He took the real best from it, bringing in most of the TV programs in a free tax system wich conveys 243 billions of Lire net.

Maccanico Law (1997)

Based on the ruling by the Council for December 7, 1994, the Mammi law that allows the Fininvest to own three analogue TV networks is unconstitutional:

Rete 4 TV chanel, must be turned off and to switch on the satellite, by August 28, 1996,

But the Minister of Posts and Telecommunications of the Prodi government, Antonio Maccanico, grant an extension until December 31, 1996 pending legal "system". At year end, nothing was done to reform and there were a further extension of six months. In July 24, 1997, at last the law Maccanico: the editors of TV, as established by the Advisory Body, may not hold more than 20% of national frequencies available, so a network Mediaset is too many. But to enforce the new roof will provide the Authority for Communications (Agcom), which will become active only when they exist in Italy "a reasonable development of the users of television programs by satellite or cable." What it means to "reasonable development" nobody knows, so Rete4 will continue to transmit indefinitely.

D'Alema Saving Rete 4 (1999)

The new company Agcom sprang into action in 1998, presenting a new plan for television frequencies, including eight national TV licenses. Rete4, being "excessive" according to Maccanico, lost the grant, which went to Europa7's Francesco Di Stefano. However, in 1999, the D'Alema government granted Rete4 a "provisional authorization" to continue to transmit without a license. As a result, for ten years, Europa7 would be denied the frequencies which it was entitled to by law.

Gip-Gup (1999)

Berlusconi and Previti, charged with bribing judges in Rome (Mondadori processes, Sme-Ariosto, and Imi-Sir), want to eliminate the investigating magistrate in Milan Alessandro Rossato, who signed the arrest of corrupted judges and lawyers in Fininvest Pacifico and Acampora. He was the one who has also ordered the arrest of Mr Previti (blocked by the Camera, when the "Ulivo" coalition had the power as majority parties).

49

At the present it is up to Mr. Rossato, as the Gup, to conduct preliminary procedures of the three processes and to decide on the claims made by Milan prosecutors.

The processes began in 1999.

On a proposal by Mr. Guido Calvi, the lawyer of Massimo D'Alema, the left-centre passes a law that makes incompatible the figure of Gip to the judge of the preliminary hearing: the judge who followed the preliminary investigation can no longer follow the preliminary hearing. He has to takeover it to a colleague wich obviously does not know the documentation with a huge loss of time. As a result the preliminary hearing with regard the Imi-Sir and Sme process, already started in front of Mr. Rossato, continue under its management and they will be closed at year-end with the indictments of the defendants. Instead, the one regarding Mondadori, wich is not even started, is immediately switched to another judge, Mr. Rosario Lupo, who acquits all defendants for lack of proofs (afterward, on appeal of the Prosecutor, the Court of Appeal judgment will return all of them, except one: Silvio Berlusconi, who is called prescribed due to general extenuating circumstances) . . .

Letters of Request (2001)

Back in 2001 at Palazzo Chigi, Berlusconi immediately passed a law barring Italian prosecutors from using any evidence coming from abroad. This, of course, included evidence that demonstrated corruption on the part of Roman judges. For months, Previti's lawyers asked the court to discard pages of evidence from the Milan Swiss bank showing transfers, either because there were no page numbers, because they were photocopies without stamps of authenticity, or because they were handed directly to the Italian judges without passing through the Ministry of Justice. The court consistently had rejected those demands, but now it became state law.

With the justification of ratifying the convention between Italy and Switzerland in 1998 for mutual legal assistance (which the centre had conveniently forgotten for the three previous years), on 3 October 2001, the CDL(Casa delle Libertà) Law 367 was enacted, invalidating any evidence submitted by foreign court that was not original or authenticated with a special stamp. Invalidated were documents that were faxed, delivered by mail, delivered by hand, photocopied, or containing some defect on the form. Although the defendants never objected to the authenticity of the documents used in the case, they were all discarded. Thankfully, the courts have since found that the law contradicts all international conventions.

False Accounting (2002)

Since Berlusconi had five ongoing trials for false accounting, on 28 September 2001, the majority approved Proxy Law No. 61, instructing the government to reform corporate crimes. Beginning in 2002, new laws would establish new maximum terms of four or five years for listed companies and three years for non-listed companies (compared to seven years and four years, respectively). Making false claims for an unlisted company was only punishable upon the complaint of a shareholder or creditor. The law also decriminalized certain offenses (such as submitting a false budget to banks) and set very broad thresholds for what was now permissible (for false accounting to be an offense, it would have to exceed 5 per cent of operating income, 1 per cent of equity, and 10 per cent of evaluations).

Consequently all the processes against Berlusconi for false bookkeeping are deleted: either because there is not a lawsuit against the shareholders (Berlusconi does not complaint Berlusconi), either because this particular false accounting does not exceed the percentage, wich is set by law, or just because the new law, thanks to a hasty prescription, extinguishes the offense.

European Arrest Warrant (2001)

Among the European Union, the second Berlusconi government was the only one that refused to ratify the "European arrest warrant," but only with respect to crimes against financial institutions and public administration. According to *Newsweek*, Berlusconi was "afraid of being arrested by the Spanish courts" for the Telecinco investigation. Italy began to apply in their territory the "European arrest warrant", only on april 22/2005. While other European countries began to Apply the Law August 7, 2002

The Government Moves the Court (2001)

On 31 December 2001, while Italians were celebrating the New Year, Justice Minister Roberto Castelli, at the request of Previti's attorneys, denies any procedure against the extension in court to Judge Guido Brambilla, a member of the board that leads the process Sme-Ariosto. He has its "immediate taking of possession" at the Court of surveillance where it was transferred for few months, without being able to complete the ongoing debate. Thus SME process would have to start from scratch before a new college. But then the president spoke of the Court of Appeal with a new "application" of Brambilla in court until later this year.

Cirami (2002)

Berlusconi and Previti's defenders contended that the Supreme Court should move the latter's trial to Brescia, since, they argued, the entire Court of Milan was prejudiced against them. To enhance their chances even further, they reintroduced the old notion of "legitimate suspicion", the current time, when he moves to the uncomfortable process "Port of Shadows". And 'the law Cirami 248, approved the final 5

November 2002. But even this does not works: the Supreme Court, in January 2003, rejected the request to move, declaring the Court of Milan to be serene and impartial.

Maccanico-Schifani (2003)

The beginning of the process to Silvio Berlusconi about Mondadori and SME, are close

And 'the law Cirami 248, approved the final 5 At the suggestion of Senator Margaret Antonio Maccanico, on 18 June 2003, CDL(Casa delle libertà) Law 140 was approved (first signatory Renato Schifani), indefinitely suspending the processes to the Presidents of the Republic of the House, Senate, Council and the Constitutional Court. Court of Milan blocks the processes waiting to Berlusconi that session to examine the exceptions of unconstitutionality raised. And out again in January 2004, when the Court rejected the "award".

Former Cirielli (2005)

On 29th November 2005 enacts the law ex Cirielli CDL (unrecognized by his own proposer), which limited prison sentences for those over seventy years of age (coincidentally, Previti and Berlusconi had just turned seventy). The law brings the crimes prescribed from 100.000 to 150 000 per year, tenth the charges of Mediaset's process (offenses to tax evasion is reduced from 15 years to 7 ½ years), and destroy the Mills trial (even judicial corruption is no longer prescribes in 15 years, but in 10 years).

Tax Amnesty (2002)

The Finance Act 2003 enacted in December 2002 contains an amnesty clause that Berlusconi vowed neither he nor his companies would ever use. However, Mediaset advantage of the law to avoid paying 197 million Euros charged by Inland Revenue, paying just 35 million Euros. Berlusconi also used the amnesty clause to pay just 1800 Euros instead of 301 billion lire challenged by prosecutors in Milan.

Note:

Now I ask myself a question: but with such laws, amnesties, pardons or anything else, who would not be tempted to evade taxes, especially those in large retailers, merchants and industrialists who have a big business? With such absurd laws that are approved in Italy, how do you expect, that there is social fairness? The more I advance in my research, the more I realize what a crazy country is Italy.

And I repeat again: if Italy has 2,000 billion Euros of debt, because it lacked the seriousness of the Italian governments in the last 50 years. Are inconceivable amnesties or prescriptions, for offenses against public administration and against the State, but have always been approved by all the Italian political parties.

Amnesty for Defendants (2003)

On 24 June 2003, with Decree 143, alleged "authentic interpretation" of the amnesty, the government puts us even those who have "contributed to commit crimes," even if they have not signed the fraudulent misrepresentation. That is, the Berlusconi government also saves the 9 co-accused the prime minister, accused in the process of helping him to escape Mediaset with false or inflated invoices.

Pecorella (2006)

Saved from prosecution in the SME trial due to "extenuating circumstances," Berlusconi feared that the appeal would be withdrawn, resulting in his condemnation. So in 2005, his lawyer, Gaetano Pecorella, Chairman of the House Judiciary, approved a law abolishing the appeal. According to the new law, prosecutors can not appeals in case of acquittals or prescriptions. If convicted on his first instance, however, the defendant can still appeal. President Ciampi rejected as unconstitutional the Pecorella law. Berlusconi makes longer the deadline of the legislature to re-approve it and resubmit the same one. (Law n. 46) in January 2006. Ciampi is forced to sign it this time. But then the ball View as unconstitutional

Frattini (2002)

On 28 February 2002, the CDL Frattini law on conflict of interest was approved. The law states that those in government who own businesses but are "mere owners" are not in conflict of interest and will not be forced to sell them. This had only one consequence for the Prime Minister: he had to give up the presidency of AC Milan, his football team.

Gasparri 1 (2003)

Under the new ruling of the Look of 2002, by 31 December 2003, Rete4 would have to be switched to satellite. On 5 December, the CDL approved the Gasparri television law: Rete4 could continue to pass "even though no facilitation", i.e. even if no longer has the concession since 1999. The antitrust limit of 20 per cent ownership would now be calculated based on fifteen stations instead of ten (including Telemarket). Berlusconi could therefore keep his three Mediaset television stations. As for the 20 per cent limit, even this has been raised through the trick of "Sic", which includes a panel so wide of countless situations. Confalonieri and Mediaset would be able to expand estimated revenues by €1-€2 billion per year. However, on 16 December, 2003 the law was ruled unconstitutional.

Berlusconi Saves Rete 4 (2003)

With two weeks to go until Rete4 was set to turn out the lights, on Christmas Eve, Berlusconi signed a Decree 352, saving Rete 4, which would grant an extension of six months, pending the new Gasparri ruling.

Gasparri 2 (2004)

The new law passed on 29 April 2004, very comparable to that rejected by the Quirinal, insured that Rete4 would not be in breach of antitrust limits, because by 30 April 50 per cent of Italians would be receiving a digital terrestrial signal, which would provide them with hundreds of new channels. However, to date, only 18 per cent of the population receives the digital signal. Agcom offered a broad explanation of the standard, considering an area "totally digitized" as long as service is available to a single user in that area. Rete 4 was saved, and Europe7 channel does not have frequencies in order to trasmit thear programs

State Decoder (2004)

To inflate the area of digital, the Berlusconi's Government with the "finanziaria law" 2005, approved in December 2004 provided government grants of €150 in 2004 and €70 in 2005 for those who bought TV decoders with the new technology. Among the largest distributors of these decoders was Paolo Berlusconi, brother of Silvio and owner of Solaris (which sells the Amstrad decoder).

Save the Decoder (2003)

The DTT was a bargain for Mediaset, which sends football matches for a fee. However, they feared lost revenues from piracy. Promptly, in 15th January 2003, the government decriminalized false accounting, carries up to three years with 150. thousand Euros in fines the maximum penalty for fake smart cards for pay TV.

Save Milan (2002)

With Decree 282, converted into law on 18th February 2002, the Berlusconi government allowed companies to football, almost all under huge debts, to amortize on budgets in 2002 and spread in the ten years following the devaluation of the players' cards. AC Milan would save €240 million.

Save TV rights (2006)

Berlusconi's party Forza Italia has blocked the draft law, supported by all other parties of the left and right, to change the system of sale of football television rights for a more "collective" with lower prices. This new system Berlusconi, would penalize small clubs and benefit only the top clubs: Juventus, Inter and of course AC Milan.

Inheritance Tax (2001)

On 28 June 2001, the Berlusconi government abolished the inheritance tax for estates exceeding 350 million Lire(up to that figure the tax had been repealed by the previous Prodi government). By coincidence, the premier has five children and assets estimated at 25 trillion lire.

Reduction Tax (2004)

In 2003, according to *Forbes*, Berlusconi was the forty-fifth richest man in the world, with a personal fortune of $5.9 billion. In 2005, he jumped to twenty-fifth place, with $12 billion. In late 2004, when his government lowered the tax rate on the wealthy, Berlusconi would save 764,154 per year, according to *The Express*.

Capital Gains Tax (2003)

In 2003, Tremonti passed a tax reform reducing taxes capital gains on investments. The reform was applied by the Prime Minister in April 2005, when yields 16.88 per cent of Mediaset owned by Fininvest for €2.2 billion, saving €340 million in taxes.

Villa with Abusive Tax Amnesty (2004)

On 6 May 2004, while *La Nuova Sardegna* was revealing building abuses at Villa Certosa, Berlusconi approved two ordinances. The first approved a national anti-terrorism plan that also contained a secret rider ensuring the safety of Villa La Certosa. The second part identified the residence of Berlusconi in Sardinia as an "alternative location of maximum safety for the safety of the President of the Council and for the continuity of government". It extended this benefit to all the other residences of the Prime Minister and his family, scattered throughout Italy. So the investigation into abuses in building his villa in Costa Smeralda ends. Then in 2005 the Interior Minister Pisanu makes clear the secret. But it was too late. The

Law 208, 2004, passed in haste from the Berlusconi government, extending the building amnesty of 2003 also protected areas, such as that which arises his villa. Promptly Hydra Realty, owner of the private residences of the Knight(Berlusconi), shows ten different requests for building amnesty. It can cure all for the modest sum of 300 thousand Euros. In 2008, the Court of Tempio Pausania city terminating the proceeding for abuse because building largely condoned by a decree merely wanted the owner of the villa.

For Mediolanum (2005)

Despite the resistance of Welfare Minister Roberto Maroni, Forza Italia imposed a series of policies favourable to insurance companies in the Supplementary and Complementary Social Security Reform (Decree 252, 2005). This included the transfer of €14 billion from insurance, some tax rules that provided supplementary security equipment (including the benefit of Mediolanum, owned by Berlusconi and Mr. Doris), and in particular legislation in 2008 to accommodate the interests of powerful insurance lobbies (of which Mediolanum is a leader). Meanwhile, in January 2004, the Italian Post Office granted a no-bid contract to Mediolanum for 16,000 post offices throughout Italy.

For Mondadori 1 (2005)

On 9 June 2005, Education Minister Letizia Moratti concluded an agreement with the Post Office for the Postescuola service, delivery and order—by phone and online—of textbooks for secondary school pupils. Publishers would not deliver their volumes directly but through Mondolibri Bol, a company that is 50 per cent owned by Arnoldo Mondadori Editore SpA, of which Berlusconi is a "mere owner". The Competition Authority considered the case but ruled that the initiative would not be invalidated because it was the Education Minister, Moratti, who signed the deal, and not the Prime Minister.

For Mondadori 2 (2005)

The 8 February 2005 triggered the operation "E-book" for the launch of which the government allocates 3 million. The companies that where awarded the contract were Mondadori and IBM: the first is a Berlusconi. company

Remission (2006)

In July 2006 the two coalition centre-left and centre-right approve the pardon Mastella (were opposed, the parties: IDV, Lega Nord and Alleanza Nazionale.): 3 years discount penalty to those who have committed crimes prior to 2 May of that yearIt was approved discount penalty, even for offenses against public administration and judicial corruption, otherwise Cesare Previti (great friend and colleague at the affairs of Berlusconi) would remain under house arrest.

If Berlusconi was convicted in one of his many jobs, this bill will save him three-year sentence.

Alfano (2008)

In July 2008, the eve of the decision process in the Berlusconi-Mills, the PDL party returned to the government approves the Lodo Alfano suspending indefinitely the processes to Berlusconi. With this law called "Lodo Alfano", the 4 highest offices of state, including Berlusconi, could not be either charged or tried by any court. It 'easy to understand that Berlusconi could only benefit from this law. In October 2009 the Constitutional Court will not accept even that as unconstitutional.

Note:

Changing the subject, you know that in Italy we have the constitutional judges who, after working 16 years are retired? And they have over 15,000 Euros a month pension, and are entitled to have the car and driver paid by the Italian state until their death? And the Italian state pays for everything that concerns the maintenance of the car? It's not a joke. Reader, I'm not writing a book concerns of jokes, although it seems.

More VAT for Sky (2008)

On 28 November 2008, the government doubled the taxes on Sky's pay-TV services, owned by Rupert Murdoch, the main competitor of Mediaset, bringing them to 10-20 per cent.

Less Commercials for Sky (2009)

On 17 December 2009, the Berlusconi government launched the Roman decree requiring Sky by year 2013 to fall from18- to 12 per cent of the hourly spot.

More Shares (2009)

Is enacted into law that allows a company to increase ownership of the shares of his company from 10 to 20 per cent. This was how Fininvest increased its control of Mediaset.

The Legitimate Impediment (2010)

Not knowing how to stop processes and Mills Mediaset, Berlusconi is 10 March 2010 approved a law that automates the "lawful impediment" to appear at hearings for himself and his ministers, all for a period of six months, extended up to 18. Just a certification of the Presidency of the Council and the judges will have to stop, without being able to check if the impediment is effective and legitimate. All pending the final solution, that is, the new ad personam laws that will bring the total to 40 quotes: "short process" anti-wiretapping and a constitutional-Lodo Alfano. That is unconstitutional.

For all these laws designed to save and enrich Berlusconi, we must thank the politicians of the Prodi government during the period 1996-2001. Many people, like me, voted for the Berlusconi coalition in elections following 2001. Please see that, thanks to the left, foreigners have an advantage compared to Italians with respect to the allocation of housing, municipal kindergartens, and many other areas. This cannot help but make people angry. Of course I did wrong more Bossi's Northern League leader, who remained an ally without obtaining benefits for those who vote him.

Since 2001, the people of northern Italy have greatly anticipated Fiscal Federalism, a law that would allow the riches produced in the territory to remain in the territory. But now everything goes to Rome, where the government, as a good father, redistributes our riches throughout the country, especially in south, where for many people work is something to be strictly avoided. Yet after ten years it still has not been approved. Moreover, between 1996 to 2006, both the Prodi coalition and Berlusconi were not able to approve reforms that would have been approved in any civilized country already. Corporations remain too powerful, and no one has had the honesty, for the good of the country, to make any laws against them.

Chapter 6

La lega Nord (The Northern League) and his Leader and Founder Umberto Bossi

The Northern League was born from the needs of the population of northern Italy, so their voices could be heard against the ongoing injustices committed by the Roman government. After the end of the" years of lead "(1970 to 1980, years in which left-wing terrorists killed dozens of people) in the north, many small parties arose that looked to address the needs of local people not in Rome, places to distant for the government to address their needs. The strength of the Northern League was the unification of all these local desires, which had nothing to do with power or personal enrichment but simply human rights, so that the people would not be forced to work and pay taxes to Rome.

The people of the north do not discriminate against anyone. Although it is true that some supporters of the league are extreme in their statements, this is because each person has his own individual character. What matters is that the league has done a lot to bring politics to the people, which unfortunately was not the case in the years before

1989 in Bergamo (Lombardy region), the Statute of the Northern League was established. This new political party was formed from the merger of the Lombard League, of which Bossi was the founder, and all the other leagues in northern and central Italy, including Piedmont Autonomist, Liga Veneta, Union Liguria, League Emilia-Romagna, and Tuscany Alliance. The purpose of Bossi's league was to transform a government that was state centric, oppressive, and unfair to the people of the north into a federal state, so that decision-making powers that affect people are taken locally and not in Rome, which could never understand the needs of people living 500 to 1000 km away.

It is normal in all parts of the world, not only in Italy, for people to want local politicians making local decisions. Unfortunately, arrogance and evil are the characteristics of most politicians, also not only in Italy but all over the world. While it is true that in some countries corrupt politicians are rare, in others, such as Italy, the main goal of a political career is personal enrichment.

The Northern League was founded in 1989 from the merging of various autonomist movements of the northern regions of Italy, including Liga Veneta (established in 1979) and Lega Lombarda (established in 1982). Umberto Bossi, former Secretary of the Lombard League, and was elected Secretary, while Marilena Marin, from the Liga Veneta, was elected President.

With the May 1990 elections the Northern League became the second largest party in Lombardy. League Professor Gianfranco Miglio received menacing phone calls from the President Cossiga: "Tell your fellow Leaguers to shut up. I do not lack the means to persuade them. One day Bossi will find his car stuffed with drugs, and then we'll have trouble. And as for the citizens who vote for the league, I'll make them regret it too. Soon you'll find that the places that are sympathetic to your movement will have more police about, and more financial audits—in fact, they'll rise proportionate to the increase in votes. Retailers and businesses, small and large, which help the League, will be passed through a sieve. The tax records will be checked, their VAT numbers will be revoked, we will never leave them in peace." Cossiga has never denied making this threat.

If even the president of the republic had the courage to make such threats, Mafia style, this should indicate the political culture in Italy from the 60s onwards: corrupt, overbearing, and arrogant, and cruel—all foreign to the peoples of northern Italy. When a person does not love one's neighbour because that neighbour is a selfish, arrogant, lying bully, this is not xenophobia. And it is only logical that two people with totally different feelings can never live together. You can not expect that people suffer in silence the arrogance of others, just to avoid being called xenophobic.

In the 1992 elections, the League got over 8.5 per cent nationally, a tremendous success for a party just born. In 1993, the leader of the League, Bossi, was implicated in the Enimont scandal, which involved a bribe of 200 million Italian Lire. It is without doubt that the treasurer of the League Patelli, grossed that amount. In fact, Bossi and the treasurer were later convicted of illegal financing of political parties.

In 1994, the Northern League, an ally with Forza Italia (Berlusconi) and other parties, won the elections. It was the beginning of the first Berlusconi government, which lasted only eight months. Bossi soon found that in Rome there was in fact no desire to change, bureaucracy in all government offices, difficulties on the part of allied parties to accept the idea of renewed thy way of doing politics, all ideas, far away, light years from Bossi's way of thinking. This shows the enormous cultural differences between the north and the south of the country. In 1995, with the agreement between the Northern League, PDS, and PPI, a caretaker government was formed, headed by Lamberto Dini.

In the elections of 1996, the League alone got 10.4 per cent of the votes, without an alliance with Berlusconi, then in the opposition. Also in 1996, the prosecutor Guido Papalia of Verona (who was not from the territory) signed a investigate warrant for the headquarters of the League, in via Bellerio-Milano. The charge was "attacking national unity". The Constitutional Court condemned the raid; since this was the home office of an elected official, it required the permission of the Italian Parliament. There was a clash between police and members of the League, whose deputy, Maroni, was wounded. It is important to note the arrogance of the police (mostly from the south) towards the people of the north.

From 1996 to 1998, the League began to crumble into many smaller movements, each in their own region. At the end of 1999 the League reconciled with Berlusconi, making it clear, what we would have done, once won the election.

And in 2000 they triumphed in many regions of the north. In May 2001 the League returned to the government with Berlusconi, in the hope of devolution (that is, devolving many powers from the state to regions). Needless to say that little was done in four years of government, not to mention that in March 2004, Bossi suffered a stroke that kept him out of politics for quite a while.

In 2006, a referendum proposed by the Northern League, which proposed changing the Constitution to reduce the parliamentarians, did not succeed. Only two regions, Lombardia and Veneto, voted in favour, while eighteen regions were opposed. How can Italy progress when the mentality of its people is so regressive? It seems that only Lombardia and Veneto wanted change to improve the country.

In 2006, the League, allied with Berlusconi, lost to the chamber by 25,000 votes, while the Senate won with more than 475,000. Unfortunately, Italians living abroad won for the Prodi government. In 2008, Mastella, UDEUR's leader, took the support of his party in Prodi government He facilitated the subsequent elections, a great victory of Berlusconi's centre-right. Now the League is still the government with Berlusconi.

aKnd Reflections

May 10 1997, at 12:20 a.m., a group of eight people occupy the square S. Marco in Venice. Some of them climbed on the high church tower to affix the banner of the "Serenissima". Their slogan was: "Qui Serenissimo in Veneto". These people were not dangerous; they just wanted to demonstrate and awaken the people of Veneto from their decades-long slumber. At nine o'clock in the morning, all the people involved were arrested in a raid that lasted thirty minutes. The day after this demonstration, despite criticism from various politicians in the Veneto region, these people became the first Venetian heroes.

On 25 May the referendum took place in northern Italy, promoted by Bossi's Northern League. With 13,097 seats in all the towns and villages in the north, the people of Padania are asked if they want to secede. On 26 May, 99.7 per cent of voters were in favour of secession. Of course, the Prodi government, which never expresses any judgment critical of itself, would go on to criticize the opinion of some 5 million voters. Business as usual in Italy.

Bossi, 28, asks for help to United Nations ONU, saying, "Now we want self-determination. We will send all cards to the ONU to ask for a real referendum on statehood, as did Quebec. They tell us that we have cheated, and then you face a referendum state. The Northern League is tired situations like this."

Some politicians say that the discomfort is not Bossi, but it is impartial, and in the Veneto this feeling is tangible.

On 31 May 1997, the President of the Republic Oscar Luigi Scalfaro, asked the judges of the courts to stop the separatists in any way possible. He even asks the Parliament to pass a law against those who threaten national unity. The Northern League leader Mr. Bossi, hearing the speeches of President Scalfaro, turn the hearts of the people of the north saying: It's time of secession.

Another politician from the northern league says, "Give us a referendum. If he wins we will be silent. But it seems that Scalfaro (former president) and Napolitano (current president) want to use force, the truncheon against free expression."

In the *Journal of Vicenza* the journalist Blacks Paoloni writes, "Have you ever asked to the chief of the State (Mr. Scalfaro) how many times the city has the intuition, that the boundary between the licit and the illicit is violated by the authorities, more or less by Roman people?"

Do not forget that the Northern League was the only party that defended the judges in 1992 when Operation Clean Hands began, leading to the arrest of hundreds of people, including politicians and entrepreneurs. Do not forget statements by the Minister Treu, a native of Vicenza, who showed a great appreciation of his people when he said, "How times have changed. No longer, as once, going to give you a tour of those parts are received consents. People are tired of Rome."

On 7 September, Scalfaro (the president) is challenged in his hometown Novara by the green shirts of the Northern League. But Scalfaro, in his typically arrogant way, responds 'If the league gets the vote against the main low,. in the north, above the River Po, I will fill the area of magistrates to investigate the rebels who are part of the Northern League.

In this period, the Northern League staged protests against Scalfaro and other politicians. In fact, the President of the Veneto region advised Scalfaro not to go into Veneto. At the end of October there were elections Po, what triggered the anger of the public prosecutor of Verona Papalia (Papalia is of Sicilian origin), who sent agents to search some residences of politicians of the League.

In January '98 in the town of Mestre in Veneto region, was born, the "North East Movement", composed of mayors, businessmen, university professors and many other people.

Afterwards it joined the mayors of other cities of Veneto. There were many people who began to follow this federalist movement, whose head was a philosopher, Massimo Cacciari.

I still remember when Flavio Tosi, of the Municipal Council of Verona, along with five people, in the months of August-September 2001, went through the city collecting signatures for a petition against the nomads. In practise, Tosi and others were acting on the part of the Northern League and as such did not accept the Gypsy settlements in the city, which unfortunately continued to arrive, especially from Romania. In fact, members of the League did not want any kind of Gypsy settlements in Verona.

The Gypsies are famous not only in the Veneto region but throughout Italy, because in their society there are too many who live by their wits, stealing and even sending their children into homes to steal, because they know they cannot be convicted. The unfortunate reality is this kind of activity has been going on for decades, so it makes sense that people have become intolerant to it. This is not racism, however. The nomads who lived in Verona would be unlikely to steal in the city where they reside. Normally, these nomads go into neighbouring cities or countries, so they have no problems with the local police where they live. We have known this for some time now. This comes at a huge social cost, because while nomads continue to come not all of them are willing to work. They value above all a free spirit and wanderlust. If we are to accept this philosophy of life, then we must accept the consequences of having these people nearby, who send their children into our homes to steal not only food but money and gold.

Less than thirty years ago, when I went to Australia to obtain a tourist visa, the Australian consulate demanded a bank statement as proof of self-sufficiency and occupation. Dear gentlemen of the various associations that help the nomadic ethnic groups, who have brought lawsuits against six members of the League, why not see the a strutting government, which calls upon Italian citizens to provide a statements as proof of livelihood in order to stay in Italy? Caritas, as well you help and defend nomads and foreign people, are you able to find them a job for their source of revenue?

I would like to remind these organizations that in 2008, many factories were shutting down in Romania, due to lack of local labour force, because the entry of Romania into Europe in 2007, caused a massive emigration of Romanians in other European countries where workers earned from 10 to 15 times more. Well, those entrepreneurs who did not want to close the factories, were forced to import workers from China and they paid the Chineses workers more than they had been paying the locals. In the Catholic weekly *Famiglia Cristiana*, there was a nice article about it at that time. Could you not arrange for these nomads to go work at home, in Romania, in factories, rather than close them?

Perhaps the nomads fled Romania for fear that the government would compel them to work in factories, which were empty for lack of workers. It is easy to accuse people f racism and discrimination, but what happens when these facts come to light?

I cannot help but think of the murder of Ms Giovanna Reggiani, forty-seven years old, which occurred on the outskirts of Rome, 30 October 2007. Ms Reggiani's only crime was taking a shorter route home that night. After descending from the train station of Tor di Quinto on the outskirts of Rome, she was attacked and raped by a Romanian, an ethnic Rom. She was found alive, with her pants down and without underwear, almost lifeless in a ditch near the Gypsy camp.

The merit of the arrest of the murderer was a Rumanian woman, who lived in the settlement illegal, Romanian citizens of Rom ethnic origin, who saw the Gypsy, with the woman on his shoulders, while he was discharging into a ditch.

The woman stopped a bus, and even though he did not speak a word of Italian, he managed to make himself understood, and the driver called the police. Within minutes the police arrived, and she accompanied them to the place where the woman was lying, then accompanied the police into the Gypsy camp, where he pointed to the perpetrator of this vile murder.

Meanwhile, another police car arrived, and the nomads in the field showed their intolerance towards the police. Two policemen, after finding personal victim's belongings in the cabin of the accused, arrested the alleged offender and took him to jail.

A Senator for the PRC (Communist Party of refunding), Salvatore Bonadonna, went to see the conditions of the Rom in prison on Lungara Road.

Just days after the murder of Mrs Reggiani, a troupe of RAIUNO went to the Gypsy camp where the murderer was arrested. I was impressed by the gall of a Gypsy woman of Romanian descent, who said, as if it were the most natural thing in the world, "The nomads never kill. Steal, yes, but we never kill, because killing is not good." After all the nomads do to eat without working?

Ever since January 2007, when Romania and Bulgaria entered Europe, thefts, rapes, robberies, and murders committed by Romanians has increased. In the month of November 2007, the expulsion of many Romanians began. The re-founding the Communist Party, at that time in the Prodi government, was against the law that gave prefects of cities the power to expel foreign nationals who committed crimes. The parties of the extreme left (communists) and part of left-wing politicians were the cause of the shift in votes to Berlusconi's coalition. Why did our extreme-left comrades always protect thugs and criminals, while Italian citizens suffered thefts, robberies, murders, etc., at the hands of nationals, especially Romanians, from 2007 to 2009? These communist comrades failed to understand that you cannot defend the undefended while being inattentive to the needs of your countrymen.

As they say, charity begins at home. It must be noted that Italy was the only European country that allowed complete freedom of movement for citizens of Romania in 2007, while in other European countries, for two years, only Romanians with regular employment contracts could enter their territories. Here is the real reason why Italy in 2007 was attacked by criminals Romanians: because thieves and murderers have always been tolerated in Italy. Again I come back to my appeal throughout this book: if in Veneto, the posts of judge, magistrate, and policeman and others government position were occupied only by Venetians, Veneto would not be like the rest of Italy—a continuing disaster without remedy.

It took eleven months of continuous assaults by Romanian criminals to open the eyes of Italians to what was happening in the country under the Prodi government. It really is true that politicians will never understand people, because the former are protected by bodyguards paid for by the taxpayer, who are robbed and murdered. It took the murder of Mrs Reggiani to realize the seriousness of the situation. In fact, soon after, in Bruno Vespa's Porta a Porta(*Door to Door*) on RAIUNO, they discussed the dramatic story and the number of rapes that Romanians have committed in Italy.

The leader of the National Alliance, Gianfranco Fini, discussing the problem of the many camps that arose suddenly in Rome in 2007, asked a simple question: "Is it possible that in Bucharest, Romania's capital, all the camps were dismantled within twenty-four hours, yet here we are not able to do the same?" This impressed me, as I thought, and still think, that the camps should not exist. If any country is willing to spend a few million euros to equip further Gypsy camps, then tell it to Italy now, as we would be happy to have someone else accept these people.

One thing is positive: while for two years other countries tried to defend their citizens, in Verona, a lady who worked for a cooperative cleaning company was told just before Christmas of 2007, "Lady, next year I cannot pay more than 5 euros per hour. If you do not like to remain at home, I already have those who come to work for 4 Euros per hour." This was reality.

In Italy, the following rule was never applied to civil law, but I think it should be part of the constitution: The freedom of any individual ends when you disagree with the freedom of others.

Currently in Italy, there are foreigners who work in cooperatives for €3 or €4 per hour. With such salaries, you tell me how can an Italian maintain or raise a family? If anyone challenges this, the lobbies of Caritas, antiracism groups, the Refunding Communist Party of and other parties will declare war. In fact, it is the church and the communists who have defended the rights of foreign workers to steal Italian jobs. When a country allows foreigners to work at wages so low, this is an attack on Italian society, which no government has ever attempted to fight seriously. These foreigners have a monthly salary of €150 in their country, and they live seven to ten people in an apartment so that they can save money to send back to their home countries, while Italian citizens remain out of a job. Unions have become political parties, looking after their own interests, battling over how many cards they can get while leaving minority workers in the hands of dishonest businessmen. Such a society is destined to succumb to civil war, as there will come a day when people exasperated by this situation will so many it will be impossible to keep them all in check, and to keep them from committing evil deeds, which they will justify by pointing to current events.

Is it normal, in the name of free movement of persons, that a country will allow its citizens to lose their jobs because foreigners are willing to work for much less? For years, the Northern League has been preaching these things. Yet nobody has wanted to listen. And all along that scoundrel Napolitano has talked of national unity. Yet the real problem of unemployment would be very easy to solve—all it requires is will.

On RAIUNO, this issue was discussed on the afternoon program *Live Life*. This particular episode was about a chef who lost his job because foreigner accepted less money to do the same work. They also spoke to the president of a fabric producer in the city of Prato, who stated that 10,000 people in his town had lost their jobs in the fabric sector because of the crisis. More than 10,000 regular Chinese immigrants live in Prato, while irregular migrants total 20,000 to 50,000. I ask you, who is the boss in Prato? The Chinese? Do you think that in China they would allow an Italian citizen to do what the Chinese are doing in Prato? Open up factories with illegal Chinese workers; evade taxes, things that are happening not only in Prato but also throughout Italy? Things that the Northern League has been warning us for many years, yet nothing changes and nothing ever will. This is why foreigners have taken advantage.

The president of the Prato textile factory had more to say on the topic. First, despite hundreds of Chinese companies in the textile sector, only one was inscribed Prato textile association. Also, these companies last an average of eighteen months and then close, and the party responsible disappears. However, as one Chinese firm closes another one opens immediately. This makes it possible to avoid paying taxes, because in Italy you only start paying taxes in the second year of operation. This story has been going on for decades.

From the southern ports of Italy, illegally imported rolls of fabric arrive from China, and the Camorra of Naples encourages smuggling. The ports of the South, controlled by organized crime, are doing huge damage to the Italian economy by bringing contraband from China, including cigarettes, complete with an Italian government coupon on each packet. Unfortunately, the south of Italy is the soft underbelly of Europe, because it is from ports like Naples, Gioia Tauro, and Taranto that much of the illegal immigration and drug trade takes place.

I'm convinced that if the various European countries, such as France, Germany, and others, including England, did a careful analysis of the cigarettes sold in stores, they would notice that many have been smuggled through the international black market. A few years ago, in the port of Taranto, a container of counterfeit cigarettes was confiscated, complete with the stamp "Italian state monopolies", coming from China and heading for the shops.

In addition to cigarettes, many other counterfeit goods coming from southern ports such as Naples, Gioia Tauro, and Taranto. Not to mention the port of Genoa, which for decades was controlled by organized crime. It is now established that cocaine continues to arrive from Genoa, invading all of Europe from that port. So much cocaine entered the Italian market that you could purchase a dosage for €10. With prices so low, how many young people have been ruined? And who are the organizers of trafficking so much cocaine? They are all people from southern Italy. If it is true what I'm saying, does this make me racist? To the good people of the south, I am racist. It hard to commune with people of the south, as they are too proud, and admit the reality, in many southern dislikes.

I copied a letter from an Internet blog, without changing a comma, and respect for the author, who has witnessed what happens in China.

4 July 2010 written by mr. bob

The title of the article to which Bob responded was "City of Prato, seized by the Guardia di Finanza two clandestine illegal dye."

> Useless to seize the printing works. Both return to activity after a few days' as the first worse than before. And in many cases (as I saw for myself when I was still in Prato), the Chinese are coming back to work at night in spite of the seals. One thing I do not understand where I am here in China, for minor offenses such as expired or lack of work visa there 'arrest and immediate repatriation. In Italy, there is' a report that 99.99% of the cases of no use because the underground continues to ask her as comfortable as if nothing had happened. 'Cause when a virus is identified clandestine is not arrested or deported immediately as happens here in ALL of these Asian countries? Perhaps because 'Italians are stupid for not losing face and not be racist accuse try to be "good"? That sucks the Italian immigration. That sucks, and 'become Meadow. Lawn and now 'become the sewers of China. Even here in China all giggle of Prato, Chinese and Italian. I hope that the situation could deteriorate further, so 'that Matthew and all the other clique, which had once favoured the Chinese immigration (and beyond) will bitterly regretted . . .

On 31 August 2011, there were 67,104 prisoners in Italy of which 24,155 were foreigners, a good 37 per cent of the entire prison population. Fortunately, in Italy for those who commit a small crime is the conditional sentence, that is, one is condemned and has issued, if a person committees a second offense, he would pay for the first offense that did not serve.

Of the more than 24,000, 20 per cent are Moroccans, 10 per cent are Albanians, 14 per cent are Romanians, and 13 per cent are Tunisians. These are the figures from the ministry, and it should cause those who have hindered the Northern League from realizing certain ideas to think.

I call upon those bastards (obviously, not referring to all politicians) to read the letter written by "Bob" (name changed to avoid presenting them with any problems) and see if the statement is true. If it is, you politicians should be put in jail on bread and water, and throw away the key. You cannot turn a blind eye to such things as this. You politicians are the proof of the lack of social solidarity among the people. That's why the League is strong.

Then, as to the problem of work, if there is honesty and solidarity in the social life of various communities, many problems would be resolved. Just open the local employment offices in the town halls, in every neighbourhood, so jobseekers have somewhere to turn to. These reference points, turned the factories, restaurants, etc., who needed work force. All these agencies must work locally, serving their own territory, but they can also serve as a bridge. For example, if a cook is looking for work and there are no positions in his area, they should contact municipal offices in nearby locales to see if they need such a worker. The towns and cities should take care of the people a simple system, but unfortunately politicians' selfishness and indifference have taken over.

In Switzerland, my niece, who worked in a bakery, became allergic to flour and could no longer work. For some months she took unemployment benefits. Then the town sent her a letter with the address of a shelter for the elderly. She would begin to work the next Monday at 8 a.m. Of course, in the letter she was informed that as of Monday she would no longer receive joblessness benefits, because now she had a job. A civilized country creates such a system. Yet Italy does not, because here it is the law of the jungle, without rules, where only the most cunning and dishonest get ahead. A government that never makes rigorous rules to protect its citizens can only be defined as a *criminal government*. The facts are clear. It takes time to make such a system, yet over the years it would have saved billions of Euros. With such a system in place, we never would have had the problem of foreigners stealing the work of local people, which is what is happening in this country today, resulting in a total lack of solidarity among local people. Any civil society without solidarity is destined to come to a bad end. As they say, solidarity begins at home with one's own people.

And I'll note that Romanians came to work in Italy not because they did not have work at home but because in Italy they earned much more. This damaged the Italian workers. In a normal country, stories like this would have triggered uproar. Yet in Italy, despite ample TV coverage, it is business as usual.

What sense is it to pay unemployment benefits to a few million Italians and allow the jobs to be filled by foreigners because they cost less? Where does the state gain in all this?

A lady I know very well told me about a cousin of her who opened a shoe factory in Romania. In that country, the factories are like prisons, with walls and barbed wire around the factory. And there are armed guards as well! I thought she was joking, but this lady confirmed it was true.

11st November 2011: another story. A man was working on his garden, cutting branches of the trees, with energy. He was recorded by cameras of RAIUNO TV for the program *Live Life*, hosted by Mara Venier. The problem is that this vigorous person is collecting a disability pension of €2500 a month for blindness. When the program questioned him about the scandal, the man presented a certificate of disease of the retina, which can sometimes lead to temporary loss of vision. By law, host Venier said, he is entitled to his pension and you can't do anything about it.

These are problems dear to the people of the north, and only the Northern League is doing anything about it, while people in the south of the country are too busy trying to survive using all the dirty tricks they can imagine. The two cultures will collide again, with ideals so different that it will become increasingly difficult to live together. Social problems such as work, disability fraud, registering fake agricultural labourers just to receive benefits, auto insurance scams, In Sicily, there were 30.000 rangers paid by the Region. Providentially, recently they became 20.000. It is still a massive number comparing to the 500 (less then 500) rangers located in Trentino Alto Adige, 'which of course has many more wooded area to take care of.

The Sicilian summer is full of arsons, and if they could they would set fires in the winter as well. Cheating and fraud against the State is now customary. When they are caught, they get angry, and if they can turn to the local Mafia for protection, they do.

In one region of the south they found hundreds of fake workers, among them the wife of a famous lawyer. The judge questioned why she was involved in the scandal, and she said that she liked to go to work. Even the rich, if they can, cheat the State. It seems now to be a social disease—southern syndrome, if you will. We joke at work about this, but it's a fact that there isn't a day that goes by where you don't hear such a story on the radio or in the newspapers.

Frankly, I see no remedy for such conduct, and if this continued for decades, as it has since the 70s, it means that the cheaters are being protected.

July 2009, Verona. The judiciary has closed the process eight years after that infamous petition in 2001 urging people to sign to "get rid of the Gypsies from Verona" and "dismantle settlements and the non-realization new Rom camps."

The Court of Cassation finally confirmed the sentence imposed by the Court of Appeals of Venice against Flavio Tosi and five other members of the Northern League for having "promoted racism" and violating the Mancino law against discrimination. When the process concluded, the mayor of Verona, Flavio Tosi, said, "This is a process that in a normal country would not even have started, but it has cost the

Italian taxpayer good money." The Chief Justice has said it no longer appealed the sentence to two months against the mayor of Verona, Matteo Bragantini deputato, Vice President of the Province of Luca Coletto, municipal councilor Enrico Coursi, the leader of the Northern League in council municipal Barbara Tosi and current board member of the Consorzio Zai, Maurizio Philippi.

Now you hear more and talk of a crisis, people struggling to get by. However, according to that "racist" Flavio Tosi, if they had evacuated the camps (nomads from Romania) and sent them back to their homes, the town of Verona would have saved €2.5 million. Do you think it is right that a municipality would spend that amount to arrange the comfort of foreign nomads with the taxes of its citizens? Who are these nomads, people chosen by God? And Caritas, the ecclesiastical body, with what authority do you say that it was our duty to help the nomads? If Caritas feels obliged to help all the disinherited of the world (or all the cunning) with their money, this does not obligate the city to spend €2.5 million building a settlement to provide for all their comforts. I repeat, this is not about selfishness, but charity begins at home with one's own people.

When Tosi and his companion reported that the municipality of Verona paid €2.5 million to accommodate the nomads, I wonder how much support the Caritas church provided (other than "spiritual"). I still remember hearing on the radio that the municipality of Milan paid €11 million to make a Gypsy camp for nomads from Romania. I wonder, what specialized tasks can these workers perform that Italians are not able to do?

Tragically, in Italy many charitable organizations have forced their way into the country to build camps for the poor, dispossessed Gypsies. It is estimated that between 2007 and 2009, Italy absorbed over 150,000 Gypsies from Romania.

In a May 2008 newspaper article, the interviewer of a politician of the Democratic Party in Milan said that he did not approve of the City of Milan always taking in Gypsies from Romania, who between the city and province now totalled 23,000. Who keeps them? he asked the political left.

In 2007, just after the border opened with Romania, the Romanian government emptied its prisons so that their murderers and thieves could migrate to greener pastures in other countries. Of course, Italy was the favourite, since it opened its doors to all citizens. History will remember 2007 as the year Italy was invaded by Romanian criminals. Not a day passed that Romanians did not commit crimes. The Northern League was not in favour of indiscriminately opening the border; it wanted Romanians to enter after securing an employment contract. However, the parties on the left have always supported the right of foreign citizens to enter Italy freely, something that never happens in other civilized countries.

In 2007 the European community brought a suit against Italy for cases of discrimination against Rom Gypsies. At that time there were many Romanians who had committed crimes such as murder, theft, and robbery. It is normal that some Italians would turn against these people, albeit too severely in some cases. I wish that these gentlemen and women of the EU would allow an illegal Gypsy camp to be established a few meters from their house—then we would see how happy they would be.

People do not discriminate for no reason. I have never seen discrimination against Indians, Pakistanis, Filipinos, or other nationalities. Why? As it happens, complaints have emerged only against the ethnic groups of foreigners who fill the Italian prisons (37 per cent of prisoners are foreigners), such as Moroccans, Albanians, Romanians, and Tunisians, who alone add up to 24,000 prisoners.

In conclusion, I wish to affirm that the undersigned is not racist and does not want to discriminate against ethnic groups of Gypsies, southerners, or whatever else. I simply want to affirm the right of peoples to defend them against invading bullies. It was not fair that 150,000 to 200,000 Romanian Gypsies invaded Italy just because in 2007 their own government disassembled camps in their country, especially in the capital Bucharest, forcing them to immigrate to other countries, including Italy. In this way they forced other countries to take over the maintenance of one of their ethnic groups, a people known to be allergic to work. Gypsies love their freedom too much and do not want to give it up; working for another master would be giving up their liberty.

Even under Communism, Gypsies were different from other communities in Romania, just ask any Romanian. That is why the government of Romania dismantled camps in their country—you don't have to be a genius to figure this out.

Thousands of workers invaded this country, offering to work for €3 to €4/hour, paying rent of €400 a month, the conditions under which no Italian family could live. This disaster is due to the centre-left Prodi government, who made this possible in a coalition with the extreme left (communists). Meanwhile, in other European countries, until 2009, Romanians could enter only with contract work. Now do you understand the stupidity of the Prodi government? Do you understand why, in May 2008, Berlusconi obtained such an amazing result? The downfall of Prodi's government, which I voted for in 1996, is due to the communist parties, which insisted on serving the interests of foreigners instead of Italians. Perhaps to them, Romanians were communist brothers.

If you are unemployed, it is not the fault of Berlusconi but the fault of the people you voted for, encouraging foreigners to invade the country to pinch your work. What I said is now known to all. This is not a war against the poor; it is about defending the dignity of the people and the right to give work to whom they choose. In this way, the allies of the Catholics, communists, and other private groups have grown rich by exploiting cheap foreign labour and leaving our people without work. This is unacceptable. That's why I hate communism and the church. The dear Church of Rome cannot take care of all the despair in the world, ending it once and for all.

71

The Northern League has always cared about their people, their electorate, and for years they have preached the danger of excessive invasion of foreigners, stealing jobs from Italians and enriching entrepreneurs. If we had listened to the Northern League and implemented their policies, this would never have happened. The problems are expected, not treated now we have caused, you know dear fellow communists? You see the Church of Rome that Italy cannot accept all the disinherited of the world on its territory?

So, dear young people who voted for parties on the extreme left, it is your fault that you are now unemployed. It is your fault that you are offered meagre wages. Young people who have always voted for left-wing parties, you cannot expect to find work easily, having allowed the invasion of the country by desperate people who are willing to work for poverty wages.

Unfortunately, at the national level, the Northern League is in the minority, and this indicates the excessive cultural divide between north and south. Yet the league was against excessive immigration, was against the camps, and wanted more honesty and less spending at the state and regional level, all of which it preached for years. If this had happened Italy would be placed very well; it would not be facing the same fate as Greece. And in truth, in southern Italy and Greece there is no difference; indeed, the south is worse than Greece, because in the south criminal organizations are powerful, and the culture of fraud against the Italian state is a way of life that has lasted forty years.

Only ignorant people define the Northern League as a racist party. The truth is, if we had listened to their advice, our problems today would be much less than they are. We must note that, today, 13 November 2011, after the fall of the Berlusconi government, the Northern League has failed in its intent as an ally. Fiscal Federalism, workhorse of the League, has not been approved, nor will successive governments approve it. Veneto's assessment to break away from Italy is not selfish but is simply pragmatic. It is an recognition of the enormous cultural diversity of the country. We shall continue to be a part of Europe, but no longer a part of Italy. We shall be a country with its own ideals and culture, free to make its own decisions without answering to anyone else. The birth of the League North is nothing but proof of what I'm saying, and that people want: free to decide their own destiny

Thoughts and Criticism

Keep in mind that although many Italian magistrates are working honestly, unfortunately, there are many who do not know the meaning of the word.

Even the Italian governments over the years, in particular the Berlusconi governments, promoted laws in Parliament that Europe should under no circumstances allow, for example, the decriminalization of false accounting. Now, seeing ads on national TV describing tax evaders as parasites on society does nothing but increase my belief that the only salvation to prevent Italy from devolving into another Kosovo is to found the Venetian Republic.

How dare the Berlusconi government release such ads about tax evaders when his own management is so corrupt? And as for Prodi's left, you should have nothing to say about it, as you have exceeded all limits of stupidity. When more than half of a country is controlled by corrupt politicians and organized crime and the other half is being invaded by criminal organizations from southern Italy, well-meaning gentlemen on the left, if you really wanted to solve the southern problem, which is now in northern problem as well, you had better be ready to go to war. Yes, sir, widespread crime, now across the country, is nothing but a declaration of war against the state. And the state has never wanted to fight this war; quite the contrary—the state has almost always been complicit in these crimes. Italy is the only European country with such a high rate of local criminals. Yet we just copy the Americans. It true that we have too many criminals. The problem is not being resolved by the courts, through pardons or whatever. In the 60s we built prison-factories, making prisoners work. As Italy always had many criminals thanks to the various gangs of the south, we had to develop these prison-factory, educating inmates on how to work. Then, when they had finished serving their sentence, it was the duty of the state to find them work outside prison, like all other normal people.

The prisoners should have been taught to work, not left in a cell doing nothing for months or even years. These detainees may have then been an asset for the country, not a cost. By doing this fifty years ago, you could have prevented the battered country we have now. Corruption would not be so high. Dear President Napolitano, Italy has always lacked national unity. From the 60s onward the only reliably consistent feature among all the regions has been dishonesty and theft of public money, in every way possible and imaginable. In that regard, President Napolitano, Italy is perhaps the most cohesive country in the world.

The problem, dear Italian politicians of the long-ago, is that you never wanted to build a civil society. Indeed, all you have cared about was getting votes, including many ill-gotten votes from the south. Do not come telling me that the Christian Democrats did well by the country from 1947 to 1995.

Do not tell me that socialist Craxi did well for the country.

Do not tell me the communists did well for the country.

I have never known envy. Indeed, I think it is a stupid feeling that does not bring anything good. But frankly, I admire and wish my country had the standards of Finland, Norway, and Sweden when it comes to honesty. Italy is too far gone, but perhaps this is the time for Veneto to save itself.

Chapter 7

Let's Talk about the South

The south will be empty in the coming years. One young man out of four will emigrate. Three out of four women do not work. This scenario is even more overwhelming than what you could have imagined a few months ago, following a 27 September report by Svimez, the Association for the Development of Industry in the South.

In a south strangled by the crisis and in the absence of policy interventions, we have cause for major concern. Just consider that of the 533,000 fewer jobs between 2008 and 2010, 281,000 are in the south, accounting for just over half the total despite the fact that fewer than 30 per cent of employed Italians live in the area. This large loss of jobs has significantly affected the national crisis, resulting in a shift of capital to other areas with the closure or "reallocation" of southern production sites. Southern industry has dropped by 120,000 people. The most famous closing was Termini Imerese in Sicily, with a loss of thousands of factory jobs and related services. In Campania there is a bus plant production, "IRISBUS" in Avellino town, with over 1,000employees who will probably remain out of work.

In addition, myriad small and medium businesses have been decimated by the crisis.

And the report shows that it is mainly young people and women to suffer the heaviest effects of this crisis, aggravated by the lack of a strategy to revive the southern economy: in the south, the employment rate of the population group aged 15 to 34 years fell in 2010 to just 31.7 per cent, a gap of 25 percentage points with the north, which still stands at 56.5 per cent. The disparity becomes considerably larger when compared to the total active populace aged 15 to 64 years.

Young women are even more disadvantaged. In 2010, the employment rate for the portion of female population aged 15 to 34 years reached only 23.3 per cent. In short, in the south, a total of less than one in three young people are working, less than one in four for women.

The dramatic scenario outlined by Svimez has raised tremendous alarms, as within twenty years the south will lose one young man out of four. This means that the south may lose 25 per cent of its workforce and the youth of that area will suffer real as well as demographic desertification.

It seems that this crisis is worse than the '60s, when many Southerners, emigrated to the North

The Svimez identifies a "demographic tsunami", which has been in progress for several years already, since the south has entered a phase of depopulation, which supports and is interwoven with the economic crisis, including lower births, lower rates of emigration from abroad, and the movement of young southerners with a higher level of education to the north and abroad. In essence, without a structural intervention for the revival of the southern economy and to solve the now century-old problem of unemployment, especially of youth and women in the south, the current 7 million young people under thirty years living in the southern regions will be reduced less than 5 million in the first half of the century.

To stem this devastating new wave of emigration an economic structure similar to the one in the centre-north must be created in the south, through extraordinary plans and the allocation of substantial public funding, and utilizing public companies for industrial progress, technology, and infrastructure. Also, we must see the revival of agriculture and tourism, as well as the remediation of environmental disgrace, rural and urban. We must stop the desertification of southern industry and create new permanent jobs at full pay and full time, under the conditions laid down in the collective labor agreement, without exception on the methods of recruitment, working hours, wage regulations, and treatment.

It is certain that the government has heavy responsibilities to the masses of the south with its governments, all the problems traditionally associated with the southern question, including unemployment, have accelerated. To put the brakes on the economic and social havoc in southern Italy, the only solution is to lift the streets to overthrow the social slayer.

Be aware, however, that since the structural Italian capitalism, the issue of the south and the tragedy of unemployment can be solved only with the conquest of a united, socialist red.

Marxist-Leninist comrades, all that is happening in the south is undeniable, and frankly I'm sorry too. But unfortunately you have not yet understood why certain things happen in the south. Just to give you an example, explain why I know all grown in Israel and the Palestinians go to work in Israel? The territory of these two peoples is similar, so why have the Palestinians failed to create a society similar to that of the Israelis? The south of Italy is the same. Let's stop with the joke that northern Italy has for decades used the south. Let us stop, once and for all, with the whining of southern professors who propagate this myth. There is a saying: different land, different customs. So, fellow communists, if the south is placed so, should the young to their fathers, their politicians, their culture and their way of thinking about life.

The south has had so much money from the 60s onwards that if that money had been managed by administrators of the north, the South would now be a better country, developed mainly on agriculture and tourism, the latter having enormous potential, with the beautiful beaches and beautiful land, not to mention the weather.

Yes, in the Northern League there are people who are too extreme—this I do not deny—but it is the communists who refuse to open their eyes and look at reality. I would like to tell a story to illustrate the degree of dominance you think you own over other political parties.

In Calabria, a courageous woman, Doris Lo Moro, a former magistrate in 2005, obtained the post of counselor for health in the region. Noting that the 'Ndrangheta had their men as leaders of local health units throughout the region, she fired them all. Thirteen new directors came from northern Italy to put order and justice to the various hospitals in Calabria. Especially sought to put an end to robberies of all types, especially involving the purchase of drugs and internal services in the hospital, which we know is a way to steal, and who knows how long this had been going on. However, the locals called the new directors "the masters of the north". This is the face of Italy's union. Continuing with this story, dear fellow communists, when decrying these new leaders, a UDC party secretary claimed, "They have called so many leaders from outside, it is an offense to the people of Calabria." The new directors lasted a few months, facing the hostility of almost all the people of Calabria, as well as constant complaints on local TV. This was the final blow to Councilor Lo Moro's project.

The president of the region Loiero reinstated the former directors, who favoured the 'Ndrangheta, and the thefts and related scams in the hospitals resumed as before. Of course, the great Doris Lo Moro, who wanted to bring order and justice to the sick in hospitals, and put an end to medical malpractice in their region, was fired. Communist comrades, did you read this story? Go on the internet and read some news articles about it. And let's stop talking about racism. If the population in Calabria had supported Lo Moro, things would have changed for the better. But the Calabrian people are too proud. All they cared about was that the foreigners went away; social justice could come later.

Communists, wake up. Instead of discriminating against those who speak the truth in their books, you should put aside your pride and listen to those who know, even if they do not think like you. Open your mind and learn to listen to others, because no one is a born teacher, and in life there is always something to learn.

When I returned to Italy in 1995, after living mostly abroad since 1979, I was totally ignorant about the Italian political situation. A year later, I voted for the Communist overhaul, part of the coalition government of Romano Prodi. Only a few years later, when I began to follow politics, I came to recognize the problems of Italy, and I realized that Prodi or Berlusconi (two antagonists) were only a small part of a much bigger problem. The biggest problem of Italy was and is still the issue of the south, to which no post-war government has ever dealt with seriously.

The facts, both past and present, speak for themselves. Just think of the large criminal organizations that have proliferated in the south, expanding to the north in later years, thanks to the collusion of local politicians. To give you an idea, I'll show a few facts that occurred in southern Italy, narrated by Giorgio Bocca, then a journalist sent by his newspaper in the south. In his book, L'inferno—profondo sud-male oscuro], he speaks of the 1970s and 80s, about behaviours that are still present in regions of the south.

There is no use detailing each medical malpractice case that has occurred in the south, for there are too many to list. The Internet is also full of videos that they show physicians' total lack of respect for patients. It is the classic southern culture of arrogance, rudeness, and bullying that too many people have in the south. See the videos taken with a hidden camera of doctors who put their hands in patients' mouths without gloves, going from person to person. See physicians who smoke in sick people's rooms. See the dirt that lies on the floor in so many southern hospitals. See the complete lack of respect for the sick by the medical staff, as if these employees were doing the hospital a favour caring for them. How can any normal person endure such a rotten culture? How can you ask the people of the north to accept being invaded by people so evil? Then I come to say *I'm* racist. Is hating evil, disrespectful behaviour racist? If so, then I am proud of it, because I do not want to see people who are evil working in hospitals in my country, in Veneto.

As for you, people of the south, perhaps if you paid more attention to the golden rule—do unto others as you would have them do unto you—your region wouldn't be in such bad shape. Seeing videos on the Internet depicting what is happening in your hospitals, how patients are treated, how huge resources of money are wasted, how private hospitals are committing scams against regional health boards for money, the continued failure of almost all public institutions, I cannot help but think that you have been the cause of your own problems.

It is unnecessary to blame the State, or the governments of the centre-right or centre-left, because there are people in government elected by you who are part of your own territory, whom you defend from criticism, yet these are the first to commit injustices towards their own people.

When you read that 99 per cent of insurance fraud against the state, much of it involving false agricultural labourers receiving unemployment benefits, occurs in the South, it makes us understand the extent of the problem. There's so much fraud in Naples that it has been proposed that it enter the Guinness Book of Records as the world's most fraudulent city when it comes to auto insurance. This is not to say that all Neapolitans defraud insurance companies; however, are those statistics.

Even when fraud occurs in the North, as in Friuli Venezia Giulia, in the city of Udine, is usually perpetrated by a gang of crooks of Neapolitans. Some will call me racist for saying this, but the facts speak for themselves. Of course there are also scammers in the north, but there is a limit to the amount of scammers there.

As for public institutions such as schooling, never in my part of the country would you see the evaluations of cunning professors who give high marks to certain students regardless of performance so that they can easily find work with their diplomas in hand. This great injustice to the students of the north, which continued for decades, has produced public managers from the South that are incompetent, dishonest, and arrogant, because those who bought their degree certainly will not be honest when they enter the world of work. The fact remains that there are also many deserving southern students, but unfortunately these are few, as those who jockey for position corruptly hold all the power. All Italian institutions, and all of Europe, know how easy it is to get a diploma in the South. This is an enormous loss to society that no politician wants to address seriously, yet it should have been addressed at least thirty years ago. Now the damage has been done, not only culturally but also economically, and that damage is incalculable.

Now all of Italian society, even the north unfortunately, is infected with a deadly virus that will be difficult to eradicate. Having everything come so easily, with public institutions so corrupted that there is no real competition for any job in the state, has become a habit. This never could have happened in any other European country, but it is standard practise in Italy.

Lack of conscience, haughtiness, and dishonesty is now cultural baggage of this nation. Politicians and executives in all public institutions, by ensuring that Italy remains together, has also ensured its inevitable economic collapse. We now live in an absurd situation where the North is expected to produce and work, while the South, producing incompetent managers, as well as police, financial officers, and army, reaps the benefits. Such a tradition cannot continue.

On the night of 12 November 2011, I read a number of e-mails criticizing the League. Reading those e-mails I could not help but note one thing: the south will never change. Whenever there has been an article critical of misdeeds in the South, I have never read an answer by a Southerner affirming the article. I have never read them said, "It's true, and we need to change our mindset."

I am proud, just as they are, but as long as they defend the politicians that rob them, the country will never improve. I as a Venetian citizen, I cannot allow that to happen. That's why I've written this book.

Chapter 8

Lazio

When one speaks of Rome, one cannot overlook the Vatican an independent State. The Vatican has combined so many, and on principle, I must at least mention their past misdeeds. Religion aside, the Vatican is made up of normal people like all of us, and with the same proclivities for corruption. It is unrealistic to think that all priests are honest. Here is an assortment of headlines criticizing the church from newspapers across the political spectrum:

Violation of the law against money laundering and bank accounts suspected of fifty

The Vatican Bank to serve the "clique of contracts"

Rome and Perugia investigating the shady relationship between the IOR(Vatican city bank) and the "gel system" that ruled the big contracts and handing out bribes, favours and gifts to politicians and officials.

Ties emerge to say the least disturbing of the investigation of Perugia that investigates the "clique of contracts" for the G8 and other lavish orders for "big events" handled by the Civil Defence and that of the prosecutor of Rome that has targeted the IOR (the Institute for works of Religion, the Vatican Bank scandals already involved in the worst Italian) for violation of anti-money laundering legislation.

Investigators suspect that the Vatican bank was one of the main financial channels used by the "gel system", set up by entrepreneur Diego Anemone and, former Chairman of the Board of Public Works, and Angelo Balducci to lavish bribes, favours, and gifts to politicians and government officials in exchange for trust procurement and supplies.

The connection between the two surveys is represented by Don Evaldo Biasini, better known to the news as "Don ATM". The eighty-four-year-old priest, who has resigned as treasurer of the Congregation of the Missionaries of the Precious Blood of Christ", is a long-time friend of the Anemone family. It is him that Roman businessman called upon when they were in urgent need of cash, as in the case of €50,000 and delivered on 23 September 2008, to the former head of Civil Protection Guido Bertolaso.

According to investigators, Biasini is at the nexus of Vatican finances and the "crack conspiracy" through the "gel system" consists of Bertolaso, Anemone, Verdini, Balducci, and Mauro De Santis of Giovampaola, also known as the Big Contracts. This was possible because, as surveys have established, "Don Cash Machine" is capable of handling tens of millions per year.

One suspicious transaction involved €20 million in a Rome branch of the Credito Artigiano. That is the same bank that tipped off investigators of the Bank of Italy to suspicious transactions, which kicked off an investigation by the prosecutor of Rome on the IOR for violating the money laundering legislation. Don Biasini is not the only recipient of suspicious banking transactions by the IOR. For this reason, the Romans Pm are certain that the missionary is a key figure in a Vatican-based financial crime system that drove the contracts. Not surprisingly, the same priest acts in the attachments to notices of termination of the investigation of Perugia, defines the financial asset, which he brought up "like a private bank."

Surveys have shown that "Don ATM" acted in a personal capacity on some fifty accounts, on behalf of the congregation of the IOR. These involve the Banca Intesa space (four accounts), Banca Marche (five accounts), Banca Generali (two accounts), Savings Bank of Città di Castello (one account), Italian Post Office (three accounts), Bank Carige (one account) the IOR (thirteen accounts, cash deposits in foreign currencies, investment funds, asset management), Monte dei Paschi di Siena (twelve accounts), Ras Bank (two accounts), Rolo Banca (one account), San Paolo Imi (two accounts), and Banca di Roma (now Unicredit, three accounts).

The cards deposited on those accounts documented a rotating movement of money, often for some of the characters at the centre of the investigation, including Anemone, the Balduccis, and Della Giovanpaola. Funds blacks entrepreneur Diego Anemone, who had laid hands on many of the G8 and major procurement events and would have returned the favour by distributing money and benefits to judges, civil protection officials, politicians and law enforcement, were guarded by Don Evaldo Biasini and were found in the safe of the priest. Behind is a painting depicting religious scenes, the police of the ROS, they found the safe with a million Euros, including cash and checks. The priest according to the indictment, was the cashier for payment without issuing an invoice. In this whole story came out that Anemone had done the restoration work in the congregation of Biasini without being paid immediately, however, when he needed 40 or 50 000 Euros to pay bribes, Biasini was to bring him the money. The problem is that the checks were found in the safe that had nothing to do with the congregation.

A report by the ROS Carabinieri in Florence November 13, 2010, summarizes the business relationship (bribes) from the former head of Civil Protection Balducci, and the contractor, Anemone. In July 2010, Mr. Balducci got house arrest.

The fifteen-page report filed by the prosecutor of Perugia at the conclusion of preliminary investigations on large contracts (Maddalena G8, Big Events, celebrations for the 150th anniversary of the unification of Italy), documented, using bank statements of Gloria Piermarini, Bertolaso's wife, and his brother Francesco Piermarini, the "return" statement in which both, in time, have enjoyed in their relationships now with companies related to the sign of Anemone, now with the large public commissions.

Investigators also examined the missionary activity of Father Evaldo Biasini. The Financial Police of Bolzano have claimed that the suspect "travelled in a so-called humanitarian capacity throughout Tanzania but was actually bringing large sums of cash of dubious origin to the African country." Among the documents filed include statements of Angelo Zampolini, at that time an architect, who would handle donations to political Anemone that allowed him to amass €75 million over five years of unpaid taxes alone. Zampolini would buy houses in Rome for Balducci and former ministers Claudio Scajola and Pietro Lunardi.

Note:

Mr. Claudio Scajola when he was Minister for Economic Development, had to resign over the scandal of bribes taken. When the judge asked who paid him the apartment near the coliseum where he lived, he replied simply: "I do not know. Someone has paid for the apartment, but I do not know." For many months throughout Italy were joking on the response of Scajola. On Facebook, on television, radio, newspapers, never failed that day there were lines like: "Wanted anonymous benefactor, a friend of Scajola to pay home mortgage" or "Dear benefactor of Scajola, I cost a lot less, only 60,000 Euros and I finish to pay for the apartment." Or, "I never found anyone who has offered to pay me the apartment, if there is someone willing this is my email . . ." Or "To prevent suicide, seeking desperately benefactor of Scajola".

Let's Talk about Healthcare

In this section I will point to striking news reports that show the depth of the problem which is created the Italian public debt. Without these scandals the country would now have no debt, because frankly, the income from southern tourism alone would be enough to hold the South's load in this country. Because Italy is a gorgeous country and has a good climate in summer, it attracts millions of tourists, especially to the south, but unfortunately the people of the south have have been incapable of organizing tourism to attract people to their beaches, as they did in the region Emilia Romagna. The different culture has produced a different result.

Rome, capital of Italy, is known for the history of the Roman Empire, which conquered Europe, reaching out with its legions as far as Britain. But let's leave aside the past and see how patients are treated across the region, starting with Rome. I have read various books about the intriguing situation of healthcare in the capital. I never would have thought these things could happen. If I were to tell my aunt, an ultra-bigoted Christian, she would not believe me even if I showed her the articles in the newspapers. One has only to think of the politician (who declined to be named by the journalist interviewing him) who declared that the Catholic prelates, the directors of the hospitals owned by the Vatican, should charge more for healthcare in the Lazio region, because their hospitals offered better care than that of other private hospitals.

Think about it, the writer Minerva, called the Roman health, SPLINTER LAST, KING OF THE POPE, what so much power that they have the prelates' executives.

Logically, more than some managers in the past, not only now, dear Daniela (Daniela Minerva, writer of the book La fiera della sanità-*The Health Fair*), was taken badly by the Vatican monsignors. And it is possible that the hospitals owned by the Vatican, for the same service to a patient, they are paid more, by the region?

Let's now talk a bit about the Vatican, a small state in the city of Rome.

I recently read an article dated 16 May 2007, on the Communists' webpage. In fact, in the top right-hand corner of the screen you could see the communist flag waving. While I myself have continuously blamed extreme communism for the ruin of this country, I must admit that I am in perfect agreement with the published article. This does not mean that I agree with the Communists on any of their extreme issues. In fact, the only communist I have ever really appreciated, and he is long since dead, is Enrico Berlinguer, leader of the Italian Communist Party. Another politician I also appreciated was Berlinguer's antagonist, MSI's Giorgio Almirante. The only person in the mid-70s had the courage, at the grand stands policies, to give thieves to the Christian Democrats.

Once again, it always comes back to the same speech that he would use fifteen years later to create the Northern League. If the "fascist" Giorgio Almirante (a term used by his political opponents to disparage him) had given the speech sooner, perhaps Operation Clean Hands would have also happen much sooner. My personal opinion is that the entire judiciary had been aware of the scandal for years. However, the problem was simple: no court would go against the politicians despite knowing what was happening. Perhaps this was out of fear, perhaps for money. In the South, such scams had been proliferated against the state for several decades. In Italy, it was a race to see who could steal the most, and the judiciary was asleep, or it was busy processing drug addicts and gangsters.

One thing is certain: if the honourable Misters Almirante and Berlinguer were here today, the first thing they would do together would be to administer a beating to all of Italy's politicians—left right and centre, all of them—because all are responsible for ruining their political ideals, moral ideas that politicians today seem to have no interest in.

If not for Berlinguer's untimely death, I'm sure he would've done everything he could to change the system. I remember well his speech at a rally attended by thousands of people, in which he said, "Policy is failing."

The Absurd and Intolerable Privileges of the Vatican

Each year a mass of cash moves from the public to the Catholic Church. This includes the financing of Catholic schools and universities, salaries for teachers of religion, and all kinds of tax exemptions. How much does each Italian pay per year to the State (that is, the employees who pay the taxes) to finance the black pope of the Catholic Church, Joseph Ratzinger, who is not only rich but has proven to be increasingly reactionary and intrusive? The answer is billions of Euros.

Only 0.8 per cent, from donation of Italians Taxpayers, the Vatican State collects nearly one billion Euros.

In Italy every citizen can donate 0.8% of its taxes to various associations and communities.

Of the funding that goes to the CEI (Italian Episcopal Conference), the majority goes to support the clergy (34 per cent) and "the needs of worship" (46 per cent), while only 20 per cent goes to charitable work. Among other things, this funding mechanism, introduced with the revision of the Concordat of 1983, called for by the Craxi government, contains a hidden trick. In Italy there is an obligation to donate every year 0.8% of your taxes, to religious beliefs or associations. In 2010 only the 42% of the Taxpayers decided to donate the 0.8% to the Church. What happens to the remaining 58% of taxpayers who refused to donate their share of taxes? The Catholic Church had already received a percentage of85% from donors, it will receive the same percentage of taxes from non-donors(58%).

The state pays out another billion in various ways. For example, in 2004, 478 million was dished out for the salaries of teachers of religion 258 million for the funding of Catholic schools and universities, 25 million for the provision of water services to the Vatican City, 20 million for the Biomedical Campus University of Opus Dei site, 19 million for recruiting more than 15,000 religion teachers, 18 million for school vouchers for students from Catholic schools, 9 million to fund social security for employees Vatican and their families, 9 million for the renovation of religious buildings, 8 million for salaries of military chaplains, 7 million for the welfare fund of the clergy, 5 million for the Hospital of Padre Pio in San Giovanni Rotondo, 2 million for the construction of religious buildings, which should be added the contributions from regions, provinces, and municipalities.

We continue. A good chunk of the half billion Euros of public funding for Catholic health care institutions to be present in large numbers in the field. But that's not all: we cannot forget the lost revenue for the state due to tax exemptions granted to the church, valued at around €6 billion (about 12 trillion lire). An exaggeration? No, if we consider that the ecclesiastical bodies owns buildings, used for a wide variety of purposes: missions, schools, colleges, schools, nursing homes, hospitals, hospices, and so on. Their value is at least €30 billion and are exempt from taxes on buildings, land, corporate income tax (IRPEF), and sales through the value added tax (VAT).

To sum up: one billion from Italian's taxpayers donation, plus other several billion in contributions, plus one more billion through health financing (Catholic), plus 6 billion in taxes which are not paid; the total amount is about 9 billion Euros or 18 trillion Lire, which is a quarter of the Finance Act in 2007 signed by the Prodi government.

Even more. Tax exemptions also affect the municipal government, headed by the ICI (local property tax). The tax that the ecclesiastical authorities do not pay is certified as "not commercial". This a scam, which the Supreme Court made clear in a decision on 8 March 2004, when he says that, among other things, a kindergarten for children and a center for the elderly run by the Sisters of the Sacred Heart of the Eagle, were not exempt from paying property taxes. Yet the congregation had to pay a backlog of 70,000 Euros to City Hall

Given that this principle could apply to many other similar cases, the church has been called upon to pay their way, and the Berlusconi and Prodi governments have rushed to help the Vatican. First, they attached to the 2006 budget a temporary measure to suspend the payment. Second, they approved a final measure to provide an exemption.

All that is required to qualify for this fraudulent category is for a commercial enterprise to be run by priests and nuns with a chapel in which prayer takes place at certain intervals.

These intolerable fiscal privileges granted to the Catholic Church prevent Italian municipalities from collecting revenues assessed at €2.25 billion a year. This is no exaggeration. As of 2003, in Italy, there were 504 seminars and 8,779 schools, divided into 6,228 kindergartens, 1,280 elementary, 1,136 secondary, and 135 universities or similar to universities. In addition there were 6,105 service centres, divided into 1,853 homes, 1,669 centres for "defence of life and family", 729 orphanages, 524 family planning clinics, 399 nurseries, 136 clinics and dispensaries, and 111 hospitals, more than 674 of other. All for a total value of several billion Euros. Of course, tax free.

This is not to mention the enormous revenues which the Church derives from financial income (i.e., the buying and selling shares on the stock exchange) without paying, even in this case, a single euro in taxes.

How do you put an end to this disgrace? By abolishing the arrangement!

Let's talk a little of Rome

As always, the South of Italy provides many opportunities for journalists to write books tell the stories of interesting people and events, as I have provided in the summary below.

The Story of Lady ASL

And 'out of a book-complaint Alessio D'Amato and Dario Petti swirling around the breast, which tells of bribes, in Rome and Lazio, who has taken to prison managers, politicians, entrepreneurs, and she, the' queen 'of the agreement with a private health Anna Giuseppina Iannuzzi. A story is not over yet and this requires the political more than an indication

"Suite From 6031, the Sheraton to the cell 63 of the jump Rebibbia prison is traumatic." This opens a chapter of the book "Lady ASL. The caste of Health. Facts and misdeeds," the book that tells the story. The cell 63 Rebibbia in Rome is where is Anna Giuseppina Iannuzzi 4 February 2006, from which he was released on 2 August, under house arrest.

It is the story of a ruthless businesswoman caught between relations with politicians and managers of local health authorities and hospitals. She was caught thanks to journalists who called out the name of Lady ASL. In Rome, and countrywide, news spread of bribes, embezzlement, criminal behaviour, and corruption, all under a single director, the head of ASL, Lady Andrea Cappelli, and her husband. A story that would be simplistic to bring the so-called 'malpractice'. And 'more, much more, as demonstrated by the authors of this book-complaint Alessio D'Amato and Dario breasts. The first is a regional council of Lazio, a few days ago the President of the Constitutional Affairs Committee, the second is a journalist.

It is a breathless read, exciting, engaging, and capable of provoking a reaction of condemnation to the descriptions of practises and rituals that took place between Lady ASL and politicians and managers of local health services, particularly between ASL B and ASL C of Rome. Millions of euros swirled, passing from hand to hand, between politicians and managers, which, in turn, assured the structures of regional funding for Lady ASL performance ever delivered. It reads like a officer novel, taking place in one of the most luxurious hotels in the capital, the Sheraton on the skating Eur, where Lady ASL resided in the most elegant of suites, room 6031, where politicians and managers came to do business and to collect wads of hundreds of millions of euros.

A tour of 'heavy', with meetings taking place even with excessive confidence, it was so strong in security protagonist impunity. Despite their initial feelings of omnipotence, when one by one they ended up in prison they began to speak, revealing the colossal dimensions of fraud against the Lazio region and public health.

In addition to several managers within the tight loop of Lady ASL, justice went after several councillors, politicians at the top of the majority centre-right, led by former President Francesco Storace, who still has not been caught in net Lady Asl, although raised by herself and by the councilors of the time, involved in the investigations: Giulio Gargano, Giorgio Simeoni, Mark Verzaschi. Also making their appearance in connection with Health Lazio was Daniela Di Sotto, former wife of Gianfranco Fini (leader of the political party National Alliance), and the ever-present Ciarrapico Giuseppe, an old acquaintance of politics, finance and the courtroom Italic. The investigations and convictions were placed in the hands of four judges: the PM's anti-Mafia Directorate in Rome Giovanni Bombardieri, and Giancarlo Capaldo, the GUP Adele Rando, Maria Teresa Covattathe GUP.

In 2005 Lady ASL's operations were interrupted when the centre-left won the regional elections and the Lazio region cut the favours, in the form of conventions, that the preceding administration had granted to Lady ASL. The Lazio Region, led by Piero Marrazzo, even brought civil proceedings against her for corruption, as well as proceedings against the infiltration of the Camorra and 'Ndrangheta in the region, particularly on the coast.

The Lazio region is always highest in the number of offenses against public administration, a third of which involve health. These two facts, writes D'Amato, points to something tragically simple: resources intended for the fortification of healthcare are diverted to other purposes. In Lazio, money stolen from the community has led to an unprecedented debt of €9.6 billion. And here we are today where the Lazio Region is committed, together with the Government, in are payment plan of health deficits.

Good manager, when detached from politics, more controls, a new governance system, oriented towards the customer satisfaction at last. Are some steps you cantake the policy from the beginning, indeed, would have had to do because "everyone must do his part, concluded Alessio D'Amato—in the belief that we are dealing with a delicate step: reform the system or download failures to future generations."

This is the classic scam, and very easy to do in the absence of controls, and in Italy, according to Ministry of Health data, there are no controls over 2.5 per cent. In a country so corrupt, how could controls be so low? Who has made the decision the to set them that way? Maybe the politicians?

The police investigation in Rome led to the arrest of nine people for fraud of the regional health service amounting to €5 million. These involved the administrative director of the ASL and employees in a single hospital. The scam was simply to charge for more meals than were actually provided. The same was done with bedding, etc. In short, hospital administration took money for services rendered in addition to those that were not.

Without controls, it is rational that such things will happen, and in more dishonest parts of the country, this will lead to tragedy. There are also dishonest people in the North, as there are no doubt dishonest people in Switzerland and Germany, but there is a great chasm between these regions and southern Italy. Which European country (excluding those to the east) is similar to the South? Denmark, Sweden, Holland?

When Lady ASL was arrested in 2005, she began to name all the other great entrepreneurs involved in the healthcare scam. She even became angry, saying that the judiciary would take only people like you, and not entrepreneurs, who were protected by politicians. Of course, having been caught red-handed, she soon began to talk, confessing to everything. Thanks to her confessions, more than ninety people were arrested after 2005. Of course, not all were reported.

In Italy, repentance pays well. They know the repentant Mafia, a figure that costs to the community. Later, the owner of Tosinvest, Gianpaolo Angelucci, as well as his father Antonio (a member of the PDL) were also arrested for defrauding health of €170 million. The Prosecutor of Velletri has issued twelve arrest warrants against public officials guilty of having encouraged the fraud, to the detriment of the health State.

Involved in the scam are directors, deputy directors and executives of the State, which had to check the integrity of their payments to private hospitals that treated the citizens, however, favored the scam against the Italian State with a system of false invoices for services never performed or performed only in part.

For the judge, the suspects would be health benefits never made or received refunds of analysis in the absence of the necessary and required permissions. Another twelve people were involved, including officials of the Lazio Region and the ASL. The scam, according to reports, would be implemented between the years 2005 and 2007. Some people were arrested and taken to jail.

2006 Rome

Here is yet another scam against the Health Board.

Entrepreneurs and pharmaceutical sales representatives were involved in a criminal association aimed at defrauding the national health system through the corruption of family doctors and pharmacists. In the scam, they would obtain cash or instruments for fake prescriptions, which were then shipped to complicit pharmacies, who took advantage of their consequent increases in sales. The investigation revealed a significant illicit drug trade, from narcotics to anabolic, managed by family doctors filling false prescriptions made out to unsuspecting clients in order to obtain free drugs at the expense of the NHS, selling them on the black market.

ADRIANO GIULIANO

Note:

In a corrupt country like Italy, why there was never an accurate check on the State's expense? It may be that there were inspectors who demanded bribes instead of doing their duty!

September 2010 Frosinone

Were about 150 doctors who have in the payroll even 15 thousand-18 thousandeuros per month compared with about 3 thousand-3,500 euros salary brackets ofone voice. He pointed out the nos of Latin after a complex investigation for an alleged public tax loss against ASL (local health care) Frosinone. The doctors were paid for performance "exceptional and temporary" that, in fact, should have been made in the ordinary activities. 20 suspects, including executives, auditors and members of the USL, officials of Frosinone and the Lazio region, to have frequently authorized the improper use of funds from the regional health service without recourse that the legitimacy or not to have properly exercised controls of competence on the work of the company health Frosinone.

The NAS (Carabinieri of Nucleo Anti-Sophistication) found that for "exceptional performance", the company's health spending rose from about €1 million in 2001 to over €10 million in 2010, for a public tax loss of approximately €10 million in the last five years.

December 2008, Rome, Drugs and Prostitution, Favours, False Recipes

Doctors, pharmacists, entrepreneurs, sales representatives. These are the protagonists of a fraud against the National Health Service, for a figure of close to €10 million. The implications of the scandal are grotesque: the perpetrators of the fraud not only received bribes amounting to 5 per cent of the prices of drugs wrongly prescribed, but included in the "package" were a dozen of prostitutes, whose services were offered to fatten the illegal payments. The meetings between clients and the Italian and Colombian girls, including university students, showgirls, and local television personalities, occurred in three hotels in the provinces of Cagliari, L'Aquila, and Naples. A "lady" ran the appointments. Doctors and pharmacists, as reflected in the wiretaps, after their meetings with prostitutes, contact your local network of sales representatives to report the degree or less, of benefits offerings.

Operation Apotheke, led by NAS Carabinieri and coordinated by the anti-Mafia prosecutor for the district of Rome, Giancarlo Capaldo, opened a can of worms, starting from the Lazio region and branching out to Campania, Abruzzo, Sicily, and Sardinia.

Ninety people have been implicated, with 43 arrest warrants for prison and house arrest, 12 obligations to the police. There were 168 raids and 14 requests for professional disqualification. According to investigators, the head of the operation was forty-eight-year-old Raymond Tullius Faiella, owner of a drug supply company based in Grottaferrata. He coordinated some twenty-five sales representatives, who had the task of bribing doctors and pharmacists to obtain prescription drugs (fully paid for by the National Healt Service—NHS) in order to increase sales of drugs that his company distributed. The prescriptions were written for unsuspecting patients and to people suffering from diseases that do not require the use of those medicines. The informants purchased drugs at complicit pharmacies, and then got rid of them by throwing them in dumpsters.

Rome was one of the major cities where the organization operated. And it is in the capital three pharmacy owners ended up in jail, PA Pharmacy's S. Paul (in the Ostiense area), A.A. the pharmacy on James Magnolini (Tor Vergata), and GDP, the pharmacy via Mozart (Tiburtino third). Also in Rome, three practitioners were arrested, while in Cassino a doctor and a pharmacist were arrested. All the people involved faced a charge of conspiracy to swindle the NHS.

2011 Frosinone

Financial police discovered fraud against health carried out by family doctors. Well, the Unfortunately, now the Health and its management are at the heart of current events than blacks, this is only a first exposé of a situation that will bring the NHS to declare its failure in the coming years, with devastating impact on relapse citizens. All this has led to health in the region being constantly in debt, because what has been reported above is only a little part of scams perpetrated against health in the region, committed by thugs who are willing to do anything to grab money from the health service.

Doctors continued to receive money monthly for each client, even if the client had been dead for years. Thus, the regional health services continued to pay doctors for anything. With so many overpaid managers in all agencies of the state, did no one think order the municipalities receiving the death certificate to notify the ASL? In short, the disaster was caused by terrible people. Indeed, a lot of money unnecessarily paid by health, prescription drops; therefore, who has managed to cheat gets away.

Rome, September 2006

The non-profit organization Anni Verdi, which deals with minorities and people with mental and physical disabilities, at least since 2002 would have received, showing receipts, bills never made a million and 210,000 Euros. The investigation stopped at the last minute a regional contribution to direct their own non-profit organization of 90 million.

False documents, inflated invoices, medical services do not exist and patients left without assistance.

The police made eight arrests, include Mauro Lancellotti, accountant of sixty-one years and honorary president of the non-profit organization. Lancellotti and seven other people were granted house arrest. The charges were conspiracy and fraud of the health care system.

Assault to Care INPS

2010 Rome, Twenty Law Firms Scam, the INPS

Pensions ghost, big scam to INPS. Twenty law firms targeted by PM. On the one forged signature discovered by the raid million. Over three hundred suspects many are lawyers.

Thus was discovered the big raid the coffers of INPS damage: hundreds of counterfeit pensions issued to phantom Italian immigrants in Buenos Aires. A business that involves gold twenty law firms in the capital. Now there are many Roman lawyers to shake. In many cases the lawyers have received pensions of people who died some time in Argentina. The suspects, over 300, are accused of fraud, forgery, and impersonation.

Sometimes even the State agency INPS lucky. In fact this mega scam was discovered because the pensioner living abroad made the request, the employment office of a document, strange coincidence, there was in the same office with the same name, another request. Soon they realized that the signatures were diverse, so what was advised of the Guardia of Finanza, which, with the later investigations, came to the demonstration in the capital were many more scams. Just think, the Finance found that there was ever done any confirmation if it was right, and regularity for the request of the retirement pension.

Here's How You Can Destroy a Civil Society

For the INPS(National Social Security Institue) is a hard blow. The Constitutional Court guarantees a monthly disability allowance even to non-EU foreigners—not just to those who after five years have obtained permanent residents, but to all those who qualify (wich does not mean they are illegal immigrants) and may not work for a handicap. So while the government and Parliament, deal with the crisis squeezing the welfare state of the Italians are trying to save money by reducing subsidies for the handicapped. Well, there is no savings in trying to avoid giving money to all foreigners who arrive in Italy.

The problem has grown so serious that there is now the risk of "benefits tourism" in Italy, with the arrival of foreigners who know how to fake disability so that they can be maintained at public expense, without working.

Fifteen Constitutional Court judges have already taken the decision, although not yet public. There was a split during meetings at the Palace of the Council, but in the end the majority allowed the appeal in the Court of Appeal of Turin, declaring the provision granting the disability allowance unconstitutional, in Italian, EU and non-EU citizens only if the holders of residence permits.

Now I understand why foreigners are so fond of Italy. A country so full of dishonest and stupid people is hard to find.

Let me conclude this brief chapter on the Lazio region by recalling the words of current mayor of Rome, Gianni Alemanno, who said that his region pays 35 billion euros in taxes every year. About it, I shall remember that if his region pays so many taxes to the State, it's because in Rome there are all the ministries, with tens of thousands of employees, not counting the four thousand leaders of ministries and other public bodies

Not to mention State-owned companies with headquarters in Rome. This monopoly says a lot about it. The Northern League continues to talk about federalism. Well, the Roman state is the first to have implemented federalism, having held in its territory the headquarters of all State-owned companies. Not to mention the national airline Alitalia, which failed due to the callous centralism of the Roman state, having allowed only to the people of Latium to have benefits over other Italian citizens. Just think of the bankrupt Alitalia after it cost billions of Euros to Italian taxpayers. I still remember that 86 per cent of Alitalia employees were residents in Rome. The crew that did the Milan-New York line were taken from their homes in Rome (by Alitalia minibus), taken to the airport to catch the plane to Milan. I wonder if, now that Alitalia is privately owned, there are still costs like that.

Waste, in all areas of the state, continued for decades, and fraud suits continue in state agencies like the secret service, whose leaders were tried for being in possession of significant amounts of money, making it necessary to audit the agency figures. Just do a search on the Internet to learn of the many misdeeds in Rome against the state and its agencies. On the other hand, do not forget that the Roman Empire fell because of too much corruption, where he came to be a competition of who could still the most. Now history is repeating itself, because the leaders in Rome are too far from the north to understand the problems of the people of the north. Selfishness takes over, because it is only natural for politicians or public officials to think of the people close to them. This disaster happening in the country of Italy, the proliferation of mafias, the social injustice, is due to the centralized state, which has never given way to other regions; indeed, it was always sought to collect taxes and maintain a lazy south. As a consequence the new southern generation is paying the consequences. If fifty years ago Italy had a federal political system, the southern problem would have been solved, or Italy would have been divided.

With a federal state, forty years ago you could have controlled the use of money in the south, because there would have been a guardian of the north. The northern regions would have checked that their money was being used for worthwhile projects, not to build cathedrals in the desert or to begin work that, once the money has been obtained from the State, is then stopped, as is customary in the southern regions. The Northern League is nothing but the expression of the great distress of the northern people, who see their money being thrown away in the south by politicians, criminals, and fools.

With federalism, the politicians of the south could never steal as they do now. Federalism is the number-one enemy of evil political and criminal organizations. Federalism could save the whole country, but it is too late, and the damage has already been done.

Chapter 9

Sicily

Costs for the Public Administration in Sicily

In 2010, the Sicilian region has continued to have an excessive amount of employees. Between permanent and temporary staff, for a total of 20,717employees working in the region. Even public managers in the region are too many, 1,963. And to make matters worse, there are also external ones, and 70 other executives. And a manager does not cost as an employee, maybe that's why there are too many. The Region of Lombardy, which has almost double the inhabitants, had only 3,175 employees and 223 executives, and I always refer to the year 2010.

The cost of the regional staff on duty, excluding pensioners, was €1.03 billion. In Lombardy, during the same period €127 million were spent. Although this data fails to take many things into account, it's hard to see how this discrepancy has occurred for the past thirty years. Even in the towns of the island capitals the ratio of managers to permanent employees is vastly different from that region, where there is one officer for every 5.7 employees, compared to one officer for every 69 employees in the average municipal capital

Regional health spending was also excessive in 2010. Although it had decreased from the year before, it remained high. They are expensive, in fact, about 1 billion and 96 million Euros, and are precisely 1,646. Just for a comparison, the Piedmont has only 144 associated structures.

Let's Talk about Healthcare

Speaking about healthcare in Sicily, I must offer a tribute to Mrs Minerva, whose book taught me many things about it. In it she begins, "For Sicilians, the best doctor is the plane. Whoever has the financial capacity travels to hospitals in the North, not only for major operations but also for simple procedures. Anyone in Sicily without a sponsor (i.e., a friend in the Mafia) or money must wait on endless waiting lists, while the Mafia and their friends are treated in private clinics affiliated with the region."

Logically, these private clinics make a lot of money taking care of mobsters and their friends. Always, writes Minerva, the owners of private clinics are politicians, the Mafia, or their friends, in regions such as Campania, Calabria, and Puglia, etc.

In the book *Health Fair*, I read the case of Mrs Angela Pagano from Bagheria, near Palermo. Trying to get more information about the case, I read various articles from newspapers on the Internet about this young woman, a thirty-nine-year-old mother of two children, at the end of August 2005, was taken by ambulance to Buccheri La Ferla Hospital in Palermo, after she went into labour. By this time the baby was dead. Nevertheless, there was no room in the hospital, and she was transferred, with the dead child in her lap, to another hospital, where she herself arrived dead. Clearly, the first hospital did not do its job, and that's why Mrs Pagano died.

The two regions Sicily and Calabria, between 2009 and 2010, accounted for almost 50 per cent of suspicious deaths in hospitals throughout Italy. In my opinion these deaths were caused by laziness and incompetence. Many will call me racist for saying this. However, during a recent visit to a dermatologist in the province of Verona, I experienced similar treatment myself. Have you ever spoken with someone and gotten the sense that the other person was not interested in what you have to say? It was the same thing in this case. I went to the dermatologist to check a neon that I have in the back, and I asked him that I was already there, to control others neon. I noticed the expression of the doctor when I raised my concern, as if I were bothering him. Of course, not all Southern doctors are like this, but considering the amount of unacceptable deaths in southern hospitals, it is clear that there is a lack of care being given to people who need to see a doctor.

The worst thing that has happened, not only in Sicily but throughout Italy, is that private hospitals were affiliated with the National Health Service. This has caused billions of Euros in damage against the Italian state (due to billing scams and cheating on the part of patients, which seems to be a national sport these days). Then there are simply the doctors that fail to do their jobs. The total damage to society has been immeasurable. The total lack of controls and seriousness on the part of public institutions in the South has resulted in mobsters of all kinds pocketing money earmarked for health services. If it is racist to say this, then I suppose the facts are racist.

Sicilians, heed the word of well-known poet Salvatore Quasimodo: what happens in Sicily is the fault of those who live in Sicily. It's time to stop blaming others for what is happening at home, because Sicily has always been governed by Sicilians. If you allowed managers from the Veneto or Emilia-Romagna region to run your services, you would now have a much higher level of care.

Continuing this discussion, I turn to Saviano, author of *Gomorrah*, that your statement in the TG of 8 pm in RAIUNO, a few years ago, are nothing more than proof of which character you are. He is the classic opportunistic, as indeed are many of your fellows Neapolitans. You do not need bodyguards paid for with Italians taxpayer money, because if the Mafia really wanted you dead, you'd be dead. How did you get permission to use national television to blame the North for the garbage in the streets of Naples? But the Camorra, the Neapolitan or Venetian is? But you, who you kidding? It 'true that northern people are not clever and mischievous like you and your people, but now, no longer like 40 years ago, now people know you, and having opened his eyes, you, your people have the courage to say we are racists?

But what do you claim, that the peoples of the north continue to be naive, when now know your evil, cunning and arrogance? Not all is true, but too many in the south are smart like you, Saviano. Why don't you ask your buddy Napolitano (President of the republic) why he never did anything against the Camorra in the 60s, 70s, 80s, or 90s. Why didn't he clean the streets of garbage? Is it not true that in Naples, tens of thousands of people load their cars with garbage as they leave the house and, at the right time, open the window and throw it on the street? Have the courage to speak the truth. If Naples is dirty it is the fault of the citizens of Naples and their ruling class, which is Neapolitan. Like all Southerners, you are very good with your tongue but when it comes to justice and speaking the plain truth, you leave much to be desired.

June 2011

A forty-two-year-old architect was admitted to the hospital Nesima Garibaldi in Catania for an easy operation, the removal of two staples applied after a root canal. From this simple procedure, the men went into a coma, and now, a year later, his wife simply wants to let him die with dignity.

Here is another clear case of pure indifference. Mr Renato Manente was operated on in 2003 by Gela Hospital for swelling in his left shoulder, which doctors thought was a cyst. Subsequently he underwent three more procedures in a private clinic in Gela, until in 2006 he was admitted to the hospital in Canicattì, in the province of Agrigento, where a histological examination revealed he had a tumour. Shortly after Mr Canicattì died despite chemotherapy. Why was the histological examination not done in 2003?

Salvatore Cuffaro was president of the Sicilian region from 2001 to 2008. This gentleman, who is a doctor, established his career in the Christian Democratic Party, and then in the UDC party, whose leader was Pier Ferdinando Casini. In 2007, Cuffaro was sentenced to five years in prison for providing information to the Mafia. Casini, the leader of the UDC, defines Cuffaro as a victim of political persecution. In 2008, Cuffaro was elected Senator in the ranks of the UDC.

In a 2010 Appeal, Cuffaro was convicted of having collaborated with the Mafia. In January 2011 he was finally sentenced to seven years in prison.

Now I wonder: how much damage did this doctor do to the community of Sicily during his time as governor?

On 17 September 2010, the television program Il rosso & il nero(The Red and Black), hosted by Mario Swinder Telenuovo, focused on the Sicily region, which, having ten times as many employees as Veneto despite having nearly the same number of inhabitants, was in the process of hiring five thousand temporary workers. Present in the debate were representatives of the left parties, including three members of the Northern League. Following much pointless chatter, a member of the Northern League made the only important point of the night: "Sicily can hire 30,000 people if it likes, but before that happens we must amend the federal tax so that each region can take in its own taxes and manage its expenditures anyway it wants. Up until now it has been too easy for thousands who have not served to be paid by the State. Under fiscal federalism, I would like to see just how willing Sicily would be to hire 5000 temporary workers."

I cannot end the conversation of healthcare in Sicily without mentioning the book written by Daniel Minerva, which claims that in any normal country would unleash a civil war, would unleash a casino is the House of Representatives that the Senate. The Church of Rome, with the Pope at its head, should raise its voice in anger after reading this book. Daniela has done nothing more but described incidents that cry out for vengeance, and even revenge.

I have already said that for the Sicilian, the best Doctor is the plane, and not only for the Sicilian but also for the Calabrian, the Campanian, etc. In Sicily, for pregnant women, caesarean delivery is common because private clinics are paid not twice, not three times, but four times the price that is paid in all other hospitals in Italy.

The health debt in Sicily is €2.5 billion (in 2008) due to the exorbitant costs charged by private clinics, not to mention all the false invoices that result from paltry controls, which are easily circumvented with a small bribe at any rate. Eight out of ten doctors have had legal problems. But do we realize that the society is composed of this Sicily?

As we have read in the book by Giorgio Bocca, in Sicily, for every euro that goes into government in Sicily, the Mafia must have their share. Everyone must pay tribute—entrepreneurs, shopkeepers, street vendors, everyone—and if someone does not want to pay, he meets the same and as Libero Grassi, a businessman killed by the Mafia on 29 August 1991. He had the courage to expose the extortionists, and in Sicily this guarantees you a place in the morgue.

This is Sicily, and unfortunately this is the South.

Note:

I am convinced that if there was a death penalty for committing a murder, most good people would still be alive. A future murderer would think 100 times before killing for money as happens in many parts of Italy. And the gangs would not be so powerful by applying simple rules: desperate times call for desperate measures.

Let's Talk about Education

In the book by Stella and Rizzo (*The Drift*), according to OCSE statistics, Italian students are among the last in Europe thanks to the students of southern Italy.

As the book explains, hardly anyone in the world is as ignorant as Sicilian fifteen-year-olds. This was written by journalist Salvo Intravia in the newspaper *La Repubblica*. Meanwhile, students in the Friuli-Venezia Giulia region are among the most talented in the world. The young Venetians and Lombards are above the international average, but the south keeps down the score.

This has a lot to do with the preparation of teachers. For years, those who failed to graduate in northern Italy moved to the South to earn a degree. What can you expect from such a system? Can the country have trained teachers and students with systems so disingenuous? However, despite these numbers, only 1.3 per cent of students in Sicily fail out of high school. In the Calabria region, in many schools, none are failed.

On 13 July 2010, the website Ragusanews (Sicily) reported that in the classic high school exam, "Umberto 1", all the students were promoted. Not one failed. Out of 72 students, eleven received scores of 100, and one girl received 100 cum laude.

From the newspaper "Il Corriere della Sera", I learned that the South beat the North about the educational level of students in school. It makes me laugh. The real absurdity is that the national press also reports scores.

In school year 2010-2011, over 100 students promoted cum laude in Italy, the regions of Campania, Calabria, Sicily and Puglia had a nice 40 percent promoted with 110 cum laude, while all the other 16 regions remained with a meager 60 percent. I suppose it's just a coincidence that the four regions mentioned above happens to be the most criminal, corrupt regions of Italy. The journalist Giorgio Bocca is my witness in making these statements, which are well explained in details in his book.

Another example: Caramel Sferrazza, an eighteen-year-old student from Castrofilippo, addressed to the TAR of Palermo (Sicily), for a graduation examination did not get 110 cum laude. The youth, attending high school in the fifth F "Sciascia" Canicattì, filed an appeal to modify the results of the examination held in July. The young man was pleased with the jury's decision, which awarded him a vote of "only" 100/100, without "cum laude", and for this reason he believed he had been penalized.

This behaviour reinforces the idea that the people of the south have a strong character and an overall aggressive nature.

Minister of Education Mariastella Gelmini should seek to remedy these school assessments, more so that she herself is aware of this (let's not forget that she graduated in Calabria while she was living in Brescia, in Lombardy). Perhaps she is afraid that a revolution will happen OCSE statistics are considered. On the other hand, as I said before, many people in the south have an overbearing and arrogant character.

I am convinced that if you took one hundred random people who have just graduated in Veneto and another one hundred in Sicily or Calabria, you would see a huge difference that there would be huge difference.

Note:

It 'a shame to see replaced the commander of local police in your village who retires with a person who comes from more than 500 km. away, which has a totally different culture than your own. In short, a stranger, even if the nationality is the same. See then that this new commander alien is unable to do their work, and that place just because he had won the public competition fraudulently, is not acceptable.

Fraud in the Field: Assault to Care "INPS"

Of the five regions of the country that account for 99 per cent of all false farm workers, Sicily is in third place, with a fake hired for every 242 inhabitants. It is also third in scams involving the National Social Security Institute, an institute that provides help to those who truly need it, and to see these criminals to defraud this human institution, a normal person would ask a ruthless revenge

For forty years such scams in the South have helped to increase the public debt.

Among the many scams discoveries in Sicily, I will report only a few here, just to show how scams that hurt the INPS are important to the country as a whole. It is an institution that is intended to help those who truly need it, but in the south it is considered a bank to be robbed. And again I say, to avoid the usual complaints of the people of the south, which could very well work in the fields, but we send illegal immigrants to work, because the locals, with joblessness benefits, sick pay and benefits for women pregnant because, for them this money obtained illegally, making false papers are enough.

March 2011

In Catania, in the towns of Maniace, Randazzo, Bronte, and Maletto, one thousand false labourers have been discovered. Involved in the scam: Social Security employees, labour consultants, farmers, and various charitable institutions.

The web site *Fresh Plaza* (an Italian trade paper for fruit and vegetable farmers) has followed the news: Italy: INPS millionaire scam, even with fake farm labourers in the list. Under "false agricultural labourers" are 48 arrested 4,415 suspects, 945 reported, 41 and 28 convicted persons on whom weighs request for condemnation. The INPS has paid more than 25 million for unemployment benefits, maternity leave, and illness. The amounts paid in 2010 or people who would not be right now defunct INPS have cost 100 million euros, according to the findings from the investigation of the judiciary on fraud against the institute. A survey has given birth to the phenomenon of false unemployed. INPS is cheated every year by tens of millions of Euros by people who say they are unemployed and receive the salary, without really being. In 2011, the Guardia di Finanza has discovered 6,500 fake farm laborers, who have defrauded the state coffers than 42million Euros. The biggest coup was scored in Capo d'Orlando, where 1759people have grossed 7.5 million Euros.

Chapter 10

Calabria

Dear Santo Versace, on 9 November 2011, I followed the program *LA7*. In all that you said, you didn't say a thing to annoy me. You would be the ideal person for the post of Prime Minister in Italy. You were elected to the people of freedom in 2008, and in 2011 you left the party to enter a coalition. Your country, Calabria, needs people like you, to address the many problems it has today. This, of course, will not change my idea that my country should stand on its own, because my country has given too much already. This is not about selfishness but rather realism, because your country, unlike mine, needs stricter, tougher laws, perhaps foreign to the European mentality, but we must accept the facts. In Calabria, life is worth very little, and corruption is the norm.

Again, I would vote for you right away, even in my own Veneto, because I've seen that you speak from the heart and I feel sorry for you. I see you in the Senate in the midst of wolves. Mister Versace, can you tell me who feels the same way in the Senate? For years, it has been said that political corruption has cost €60 billion per year, and yet the story continues, and it will unless someone says something. There are too many wolves in both the House and the Senate, and it will take drastic change to get rid of them. You should start a cultural revolution by force, yet if you did Europe would not accept it. Europe cannot accept that the methods they apply to the mild-mannered people of the north simply would not work in southern Italy. However, as long as there are people in the South with your courage and honesty, there is hope.

Let's Talk about Healthcare

In 2008 about seventy people were arrested for buying fake degrees, after which they worked as nurses in various hospitals in the region. These fake nurses even assisted doctors in the operating room. Then, in August 2009, we learned that in various hospitals in Calabria there were six suspicious deaths over a period of two weeks. "The Republic", a newspaper of the most credible of Italy, gave this news.

Just imagine how many other deaths there were that went unreported. These are unacceptable events in any civilized country, such as the death of a twenty-six-year-old man in the Lamezia Terme Hospital, where he was operated on for "acute appendicitis". Or the death of a sixteen-year-old girl, Eva Ruscio, who came in with inflamed tonsils. In this hospital there were three surgeons, not one of whom was able to perform a tracheotomy, which would have saved the young girl's life. In light of these facts, I wonder how the politicians of the north can allow doctors and nurses from the south to work in our hospitals. In the 90s I was living abroad, but I was told of how nurses who graduated in the South were not able to handle simple bee stings. An acquaintance of mine, a retired nurse, told me that the first nurse who arrived from the south in the early 90s, despite having a degree that it gave a much higher salary, had to be taught almost anything. There was 20 years ago, my country's hospital, a Southern nurse, who was the terror of the patients. She not a day passed, that a patient wes hit by a assesses, caused by the bite, performed by the nurse from the south. The nurse was dismissed after doctors got tired of hearing the incessant complaints and teasing.

This is true history, no joke.

I feel morally obliged to present some news written by Daniela Minerva in the book *The Health Fair*. As journalists Gian Antonio Stella and Sergio Rizzo, Mario Giordano, Giorgio Bocca and many others that I do not know, but they fight injustice with the pen, in the hope that things will change.

A physician from Calabria, Domenico Crea, was made famous in a 2007 wiretapping case by the Guardia di Finanza. From conversations between Crea and Mr Iacopino, a portrait emerged of a highly criminal doctor who used politics to get rich. The classic selfish person who in order to reach this goal, could cause some criminals, so they killed his political rival Francesco Fortugno. In fact, thanks to the death of Fortugno, Crea became part of the regional council, which never would have happened otherwise.

Crea is a postmodern, post-ideological political figure, able to move from right to left with ease. He has a long history of political and administrative activities:

- Provincial Council was elected to the College of Melito Porto Salvo
- Former deputy director of health outpatient Presidium of Melito
- In 1993, assumed the post of deputy medical director at the "T Evoli"
- For several years, vice president of minority of the south Mountain Community Ionian slope, where it dominates the local 'Ndrangheta, the so-called "Major".

In 2005, Fortugno managed to beat Crea by a few votes, provoking the anger of the 'Ndrangheta, who murdered him in October of that year. A few years earlier, Fortugno denounced to the Judiciary of Locri, cases of corruption in hospitals in the area. In fact, now we'll have the evidence.

2007—LOCRI (Reggio Calabria)—Conspiracy, fraud, fraud and corruption in public supplies. With these allegations, the Financial Police have arrested five people, including medical and administrative directors of ASL 9 of Locri. A sixth person is currently unavailable.

The Arrests

Former managing director of the ASL, Maurizio Marchese, 61, was also among those arrested on April 3 2007 as part of an investigation conducted by the DDA(District Anti-Mafia Department) in Reggio Calabria into health care fraud against the Healt Agency of Locri and other alleged irregularities in the management. The Gip Robert Lucisano issued six measures, while for three others have rejected the request for arrest.

In prison, as well as Marchese, is Angelo Turano, 53, manager of the company Attimed, while his brother, Phillip Turano, 51, director of Ti. Medical company, is unavailable. At home, however, were placed Antonio Scopelliti, 68, director of the Department of Surgery Hospital of Locri ASL 9, Giuseppe Martelli, 54, the service manager of the division of cardiology at Locri's Cardiac Hospital, Antonio Milasi, 68, former executive officer responsible for the school board office and the economic goods and services ASL 9 of Locri and managing director of hospitals grouped Locri-Gerace-Siderno.

Among the charges, that of purchasing products at exorbitant prices than the market: for example, 3,000 euros for an object that it cost 100. And in such quantities that even the nurses does knew where to put them. This reminds me the story of an acquaintance of mine that I took a few years ago. She told me that in the '70s, two friends nurses, who worked for a period of time in a hospital in the south, had divergences with the director of the local hospital, because there were goods in stock per thousand patients, when the hospital had 80 beds. The Director's response was clear: "you think of his work, the rest is my business."

Reggio Calabria, 2008: A pact between the 'Ndrangheta and political control of the health sector in Calabria. The order of detention issued by the investigating magistrate of Reggio Calabria, at the request of the DDA, outlined, in more than a thousand pages, the case against eighteen people accused in various capacities of criminal association, abuse of office, forgery committed by public officials, fraud, wrongful death, destruction, and suppression of acts real. The most excellent character, among those arrested was Domenico Crea Regional Council.

If you want to learn about this miserable character, just go on the Internet and read all the intercepted conversations by the Guardia di Finanza to understand the extent of his wickedness. A dog has more human feelings than Crea. How many more are like him in southern Italy? It's true, not all Southerners are that way, but unfortunately too many are.

Italian national statistics show that in Calabria hospitals, there is one suspicious death every four days. This is a staggering number for a region of 2 million inhabitants that spends €3.2 billion each year for health. The newspaper *Corriere della Sera* reports that the hospital of Vibo Valentia has 1900 employees, with a capacity of 200 beds, 386 doctors, 680 nurses and technicians, 140 auxiliaries, and 650 administrative staff and technicians, all partly in hospital and partly distributed in the territory. Moreover, in many regions of the south, the public money has always been used for electoral purposes—to maintain power, as in politics in the north. The difference in the South is that human life has little value. Then there is the southern ego, which causes things to happen that would never happen in the North. The facts speak for themselves.

July 2007: Arrest of Monsignor Alfredo Luberto. In the mid-1990s Luberto began his public service in the nursing home "John XXIII", property of the Curia of Cosenza. People began disappearing immediately, until 2009, the year the home closed, when there had been twelve to fifteen suspicious deaths to that point. This nursing home was managed by Monsignor Alfredo Luberto, who in 2007, after five months of house arrest, was suspended as a priest by the Curia of Cosenza. Also in 2007, when officers of the Guardia di Finanza went to the nursing home, they were amazed at the filth they saw—from the floors to the toilets, broken glass in the windows, patients left with no sheets or blankets, some patients had even contracted scabies. The nursing home they closed down in 2009 was a veritable concentration camp. However, Monsignor Luberto loved luxury, as demonstrated by the assets the police seized: luxury apartments, jewellery, paintings of famous painters, silverware, etc., not to mention his beloved Harley Davidson.

In 2009, Luberto was sentenced to seven years in prison on charges of conspiracy, fraud, and embezzlement. This home demonstrates how cruel southerners can be. Just think of it, a priest allowing people to live in such depravity for years. The facts speak for themselves.

In a blog, there is even a Calabrian who has the courage to speak the truth.

Here is a letter at a glance written by Giuseppe Marchese.

Difficult to administer in the south where they steal the solar panels

Yes! Is there really difference between the south and the north! Probably the thickness and importance of the parties, certainly of personal dignity and party politicians, of all types and species, undeniably quality and density of the commitment of public administrator. But certainly the trustees of the southern Italy are not helped in their difficult work on the context in which they operate. An example? Here it is. We're on the road from Campora San Giovanni, a large fraction of the town of Amantea (with more than a fraction of the average population of all the common Calabrian), in this small town, grappling with serious financial problems (like most of the towns of the south!) Made dramatic by the reported failure of the establishment which is indebted to the local authority at least 1,000,000 Euros, you try to illuminate the public road, in a serious condition of instability, at least in the vicinity of houses scattered or in small groups that are served by the same. How? With solar panels that allow the self-ignition of the public light all night. We are in the south and the sun fortunately for us there. The catch is that there are thieves who steal pole and sawing the panel. The mayor of Serra wanted to give a service and while saving energy costs and use clean energy, but . . . !

The problem is that, unfortunately, there are few Calabrians honest enough to admit the truth. However, good Giuseppe, I hope that others will follow your example.

The memory of 1996 still lives in me. At that time I worked for a company that built shelters and kiosks for gasoline distributors. Two of us were working a few miles from Taranto. I remember the evening when we returned to the hotel, shortly before, came the future operator of the distributor. He remained all night in the yard, and then left in the morning when we arrived for work. This was in the early days of this unusual device, and so I asked him, "But why come here and stay all night?"

He replied, "If you want to continue working, you need someone to guard the material." He told us that he was armed with a gun. Giuseppe was telling the truth.

For years I read the periodical *Christian Family*, a Catholic weekly. I recall one great editorial in the section "Conversations with the Father", which I will reproduce here without changing a comma.

> UNLAWFULNESS WIDESPREAD TANGENT ALSO SEEKING TO WORKERS: I am a forty-year-old worker of Cosenza. We workers in the south, including myself, to keep working, are forced to sign paychecks for amounts in excess of what we actually receive. It is a shameful injustice, yet there are no alternatives. A true Mafia bribe paid in turn to their homeland. Why do not you approve a law that will cover the full salary credit mandatory payroll marked on the current account of the employee? This would also serve to control the movement of capital! Marco P.

This letter may help to understand the divide between northern and southern culture. I have stated that while there are many good people in the South, the cancer that is the underworld is too widespread and powerful to defeat. The European laws will never, ever eradicate this scourge, which continues to expand.

The Fraud in the Field Assault to Care INPS

In 2009, Maria Giovana Cassiano, an official of INPS in Rossano, in the province of Cosenza, after the headquarters in Rome saw that too many requests came from the area about sickness, unemployment, and there were too many labourers on the fields.

The manager, Ms Cassiano, did her duty, and it was discovered that hundreds of people had been masquerading as labourers, without ever having worked in the country. When the officer did her duty as an honest citizen she now had to live under constant protection, as her life was now in danger. In Calabria life is worth a few hundred Euros and people often killed for trivial reasons. Ms. Cassiano managed to save millions of Euro to 'INPS attracting the wrath of hundreds of criminals crooks.

During the investigation of the Guardia di Finanza, a simple scam as we thought, came to light three cooperatives, which in all cases of fraud in order to perceive the benefits by INPS, were included, false farms, where they worked, false labourers. There were so many false certificates, any clever forger would have been envious.

In fields where tomatoes are produced, are immigrants who work hard, while the local people are entitled to unemployment benefits. In southern Italy there is the greater exploitation of labor in Europe: immigrant, besides being exploited it is treated like an animal, making him sleep on the floor of old houses without toilets. They are treated better the domestic animals like dogs and cats in northern Italy, than immigrants in the south.

Note:

I can make statements like the one above, because you read reports like this for years now in all national newspapers in Italy. Even on TV they did a television service just about the exploitation of immigrants, which takes place in the countryside of southern Italy.

Understand why the southerners favouring illegal immigration? There are the cultivated land is real, but are reserved for illegal immigrants who work 12/14 hours a day for 20/25 Euros. And without paying the contributions due. Now that I'm at it, before I forget, asshole you are Abbatantuono Diego (actor), why not go out of your share, and make a movie about your people? On the exploitation of illegal's immigrant labour, from animals that are treated by your sides.

And I say to all those assholes who participated in the production of the film titled "things of other world", the Venetian people is much more civilized, than the southern people. I appeal to the two southern, the movie director Francesco Patierno and actor Abbatantuono.

Sure you have the courage to make fun of the Venetian people with that film, while your people is inhumane beyond belief. I saw on TV how they treat illegal immigrants in southern Italy, and how they live and how much they get paid. They did a documentary on RAITRE on it. Mr. Patierno and Abbatantuono, go to the countryside of Campania, Calabria, Sicily, Puglia, Basilicata, to see how they live illegal immigrants, then, if you have a minimum of personal dignity, make a film about the harsh realities of the real facts. Or perhaps you fear that in your home, in your beloved south, the locals are not as permissive as in Veneto?

Venetians are not against immigrants. Venetians are against illegal immigrants who do not work, because when a person is jobless and hungry, asshole Diego, that person becomes dangerous, and it is better to send him back to his home before he goes on to steal out of hunger, sell drugs, or kill someone. Many in the South are racist, and you have shown, and you are still doing demonstrating illegally enter the country, thousands of people to exploit, because it is true that in the Veneto, there are also unscrupulous entrepreneurs, but before you get to the inhumanity of many south, it takes.

The film describes the life of a Venetian businessman, supporter of the Northern League party. This entrepreneur hates immigrants and speaks ill of them, even though immigrants are working for him. One day you wake up and there are more immigrants and factories no longer work, because they are still immigrants are gone. This is the plot of the film, perhaps made with funds from the Italian state. That's the respect that the people of the south have for the Venetian. Diego, who is free to move, not only in Italy or in Europe but around the world, but each is master at home, and if the Venetians were masters at home, you would have shot this film in your home, not in the Veneto.

And do not forget that the Northern League gave a boost to morality, which many people of your shares, an asshole Diego, do not even know what it is. Sorry for the outburst, but given everything I know about the south, for any one of them to challenge the morality of the Venetian is inconceivable.

June 2011, Catanzaro: A farmer was arrested and another three hundred people were reported by the Guardia di Finanza in an investigation into fraud against the INPS and Inail. He was placed under house arrest property was seized valued at more than €855,000. This con man, along with another farmer, simulated intake workers who get bonuses 'of unemployment, maternity' and injury by INPS and Inail.

Note:

INPS is the National Social Security Institute

INAIL is, the National Insurance Institute, Workers' Compensation

Both Institute are State-owned

Not much more needs to be said. In Calabria, which is controlled by the 'Ndrangheta and lacks strict laws, the problem will never be solved. It is a country where human life has no value, where the laws that apply in Veneto do not work. The criminals of Calabria, totalling in the tens of thousands, are not afraid of going to jail. In their book, Stella and Rizzo described very well the situation of imprisonment in America, where prisoners are taught to respect guards. They are trained to work; indeed, they are forced to work. In the past fifty years in Italy, instead of allowing them to keep their mattresses warm, the Italian state should have forced detainees to produce clothing and footwear for police, army, *carabinieri*, and Guardia di Finanza. The State should have taught the people of the south that refuse to work, to work. But this was never done. If this had been done for the past sixty years, it would have saved billions of Euros for the state, and criminal organizations would not have proliferated and expanded as they have.

In short, since the 60s, a harsh and punitive criminal justice system has been required, but this has never happened, because then, just as now, criminals were the first to enter politics, especially in southern Italy. Perhaps we would have been better off following the example of the Americans or the Chinese when it came to criminal justice. Because we did not, the robberies continued relentlessly over the years in Calabrian hospitals, showing that almost no one in this country, of any political party, is immune from corruption. Yes, there was Fortugno, but was murdered. Anyone who refused to submit to the criminals was killed, because for thousands of people life has no value. They kill to keep their territories operating. This has happened for decades. This is the proof of the spirit criminals who have had the various Italian governments of the past, otherwise, among tens of thousands of deputies and senators who were in government in recent years, there had been more than one of them, who had political appointees of this great southern problem. But no one had the courage to tackle a problem so big (organized crime in the south), and now, because of this, the whole country is collapsing.

In 1992, Giorgio Bocca, in his book L'inferno:Profondo Sud-Male Oscuro(The *Hell: Deep South, Dark Evil*), described very well the problems of gangsters of Calabria. At that time he spoke to the judge Corrado Carnevale, nicknamed *Ammazzasentenze* (The Sentence Slayer), who did more than any other corrupt judge to overturn the convictions of criminals. Despite the judge, prosecutor Agostino Cordova managed to get a number of convictions. However, Judge Carnevale succeeded in a short time, by various means, in releasing them all.

Recall the story of magistrate Mrs Doris Lo Moro. This lady, in 2005, when she became assessor for health in the region of Calabria, grew tired of the corrupt system and hired a group of general managers in the healthcare field from the north of Italy. These DG North lasted a few months before the governor, pressed by the people and politicians (the secretary of the local UDC party, Mr Francesco Talarico, stated that hiring so many people from the north was an insult to the people of Calabria), ordered them fired, and soon the assessor Ms Lo Moro had to resign as well.

I agree that Calabria has the right to be administered by its own people. But then so do the people of Veneto. Ms Lo Moro took drastic steps as she realized the impossibility of remedying the health in her region with local leaders. To you, proud Calabrian another plausible answer to that decision Ms Lo Moro!

Continuing to read the various news agencies on the Internet, I cannot help but see how drastic the situation really is in Calabria. Its governor, Scopelliti, said that as of December 2008, the health debt is €870 million

And in 2010, the finance minister Giulio Tremonti (during the Berlusconi government), sends in the Calabria region, a Generale of Finanza and many financiers, who settled in the offices of the Region, to check all the accounts.

This action provoked the wrath of a member of the PD (Democratic Party) in Calabria, Franco Laratta, who said that this demonstrates a lack of confidence in Governor Scopelliti and Calabrian ragional councilors by the Minister Tremonti.

But after all that you have read about the behaviour of people in this region, the Minister Tremonti, to have respect for all peoples, of which Italy is made, it is his duty to be checked by the Guardia di Finanza, the accounts public health?

Listen to this news (although it is not news to me). Some years ago, local Venetian TV was already reporting about smuggling of goods coming from abroad into ports of southern Italy. Then, in April 2010, in Reggio Calabria, police arrested twenty-seven alleged members of the 'Ndrangheta, which controlled significant business in the port of Gioia Tauro. The suspects were accused of Mafia association, as well as importing large quantities of products in tandem with a Chinese import-export company. Authorities identified and seized numerous containers of merchandise, much of it fake, worth tens and tens of millions of Euros.

Customs police also discovered, thanks to a mobile scanner, 8.5 tons of contraband cigarettes. The cigarettes were hidden among garden furniture. According to a statement by the commander of the Guardia di Finanza, the smuggled cigarettes from Gioia Tauro were being marketed throughout Europe. The 'Ndrangheta of Calabria has a good market share of contraband goods. Also seized were containers of Marlboro cigarettes with the label "Italian State Monopolies"' which were likely destined for legal tobacco shops. The south is the soft underbelly of Europe for all the illegalities you can imagine.

June 2009, Reggio Calabria:

Carcinogenic Chinese Shoes Seized by the Guardia DI Finanza.
by Pino D'Amico

A joint operation between the Company ready to use the Guardia di Finanza and Carabinieri Company, currently in progress throughout the country and whose developments are still unpredictable, has allowed us to identify and withdraw from the market a large amount of shoes produced and imported from China. Careful laboratory analysis of footwear showed that it contained a quantity of hexavalent chromium, carcinogenic and harmful to human health, 97 times the maximum permissible limits by law. In particular, the goods were found on the basis of specific control activities in the territory of a truck at the port of Reggio Calabria, blocked by a patrol of the weapon. The operating, suspicious of the considerable discrepancies between the statements from the transport and the amount of products present in the medium stopped the vehicle and requested the collaboration of the Guardia di Finanza. During the detailed inspection of the goods, although due to the abnormal and nauseating smell that emanated some products, some samples of the goods were sent to laboratories for analysis, which showed that the shoes had a rate equal to 100 mg/kg of hexavalent chromium, while the maximum permissible by law is 3 mg/kg. This can have disastrous consequences for human health, as it is a potent carcinogen that initially causes irritation of the skin and mucous membranes. Prolonged exposure can cause permanent eye damage and cancer of the lungs

The chemical analysis laboratory has also determined that, in addition to shoes chrome, there were included T-shirts, tracksuits and jackets made of materials other than those indicated on the labels required. Immediately the alarm was triggered to public health, which led the prosecutor, Deputy Attorney Dr. Miranda, to sue for fraud on the market a Chinese citizen, and require, at the same time, the seizure of shoes containing hexavalent chromium throughout the territory.

The operations of confiscation are still in progress, led to the withdrawal from the market of 5,000 pairs of shoes, many of which contain hexavalent chromium, approximately 100 thousand apparel products containing allergens harmful to the health of consumers and 1,500 pieces of electrical equipment without the required certification mark there, so potentially dangerous. In order to protect the health of citizens an attachment order was issued at national level with regard to dangerous products still on the market, and that acquired by commercial documentation may be many more hours than those receiving care to the subsequent destruction. The careful analysis of the customs documents seized at the Guardia di Finanza has allowed challenging the citizen of Ukraine A. H., who headed the transportation of clothing and accessories being smuggled, evasion of customs duties amounting to eighty thousand euros. The synergistic and effective collaboration put in place by the Carabinieri and the Guardia di Finanza in this complex and comprehensive work shows how the control of the territory on one side and the economic and financial police action on the other, may pursue only in the case in question are made in the protection of the national economy and security of citizens.

Chapter 11

Campania

Let's Talk about Healthcare

Let's hear what Economy Minister Giulio Tremonti, during a 2011 congress of the UIL union, addressing the leader of the PD, Bersani, had to say: "You seem normal in south-central, health costs twice that in the north, while making half?" Continuing his discourse, Tremonti says, "When you meet a Councillor, you're not sure if it is a councilor or a racketeer. Within the year we should implement fiscal federalism, so you can have standardized healthcare costs that are equal throughout the country to the costs in Lombardy." Dear Tremonti, why do you wish to do this now when politicians have done nothing for forty years? Another test, than they have been criminal politicians in Italy, because, having done 40 years ago the standard costs, would be social justice, which would be the duty of politicians.

The writer Giorgio Bocca wrote more than twenty years ago, "For the people of Naples, health is a luxury. It is already a difficult field when you are healthy, but if you get sick or you recommend some Camorra, or you are recommended to God." I cannot understand how, despite the fact that this critical book was published in 1992, not one politician has had the decency to remedy the situation.

Bocca went on to say, "Cardarelli Hospital in Naples, the largest in the south, works for the Roman ministry only in the morning; in the afternoon doctors are dedicated to their private activities. The Advanced X-ray departments and the CAT scan are used very little to help the 48 private laboratories."

Unfortunately, this evil culture has spread to the north of Italy, and in Veneto it works now so bad. We hear complaints about it, but nothing is changing.

Bocca described Cardarelli Hospital as a third-world healthcare facility: neglected sick in the wards, beds left woefully in the corridors. People are afraid to get out of bed to go to the bathroom, fearing that if they do they will find it occupied by another patient when they return. Many of the walls are covered in mould. However, not a single room lacks the crucifix, and the hallways are filled with statues of the Madonna and plenty of lights. Those who have money go for treatment in private clinics affiliated with the National Health Service. These clinics, of course, have plenty of money.

Besides being dishonest, some doctors, even the people are not far behind, according to the writings of Bocca, "But it is not that the poor are better in terms of honesty. For them the hospital is an asset to rob, as they steal linen, pillowcases, and tools, and an entire neighbourhood takes from Cardarelli as if it is a giant banquet. It costs twice as much to outsource laundry as it does in luxury hotels. The day of the football matches of Naples or the National, half the nurses are absent." He also tell cams continue to damage the hospital; indeed, every hospital has its Camorra clan leader, who called the law, and it is death to those who rebel, as we saw with the murder of Pasquale Crispino, master of a number of clinics, who was killed by the Camorra. As I said, such a system is difficult to eradicate with civil laws. In Campania, Naples in the head, there are too many people affiliated with, and it is natural that the fear of death is powerful in a country where killing is a trivial matter.

Based on reports contained in the book by Bocca, I'll do my research to see if health in Campania has improved at all in the past twenty years.

In October 2009 I saw a video on YouTube in which patients in Cardarelli were still sick in the hallways. When I think of all the money that the Camorra has stolen, for decades, I shudder. I cannot help but think of the words a dear English friend said to me about twenty years ago: "Every country has what it deserves." The Camorra is the daughter of Neapolitan culture, not Venetian or any other culture. To demonstrate the culture of the south: on RAIUNO TV few days ago, they were discussing tax evasion. A familiar character had the courage to say, "In southern Italy they evaded taxes because of poverty." Should the rich north, then, be the only ones to pay taxes?

Do you now see the mentality, the way the people of the South think?

In Calabria, together with Sicily, we see half of all hospital deaths throughout Italy—deaths caused by negligence or lack of skill or inadequate facilities. These data are from 2011, not forty years ago. It should make you think about the governors of the northern people, who for decades allowed people from the South, with their purchased diplomas, to become doctors and nurses in their country. Of course, not everyone bought his or her diploma, shouldn't we at least check before hiring people to make sure that they are actually able to do their jobs? And shouldn't the governors of the North do their best to ensure safety in hospitals, to prevent patients from dying? When a person acquires a diploma to be a doctor or nurse and cannot do the job, that person is nothing more than a criminal. So, dear regional health councilors in the North, should it not be your duty to check all those who have received diplomas from the South? This is not about racism. The facts speak for themselves. So many people from the North go South to graduate. It is not acceptable that this market exists—it is simply criminal behaviour.

People, perhaps capable, but arrogant, because now it is found that the rot exists in hospitals in the north. An acquaintance of mine who works at a hospital told me that once a year, the head of his department pays for everyone to have dinner at a restaurant. However, this primary is the one who ordered the drugs to the representative for his department, as he owned. It not unexpected that the Italian health system is bankrupt.

Why doesn't the region by medicines for all hospitals? And no, then how do they steal the various managers and doctors from individual hospitals? In Italy the policy is always studying the systems to steal and the way to satisfy his constituents.

We already know that Italian politicians of the past did enormous damage to the country, but we must not forget De Lorenzo (Naples), Minister of Health in the Andreotti government, who did enormous damage in just four years (1989-1993) in office. His secretary, John Marone, told judges about the bribes received in his office, given by representatives from pharmaceutical companies and others in order to receive favours from the minister. These favors were granted these thugs to increase the price of drugs, to approve useless drugs went better drugs were accessible, etc. Some have even accused De Lorenzo of developing this system of bribes. He was sentenced in 2001 to 5 years, 4 months, and 10 days in prison.

Fraud in the Field

April 2010, Caserta

In 2010, 397 people have were reported for perpetrating serious fraud against the state, colluding to obtain public funds when they were supposed to be in competition with each other.

False agricultural laborers were able to obtain and enjoy social security, such as the unemployment benefit, maternity allowance, and sickness. These scams continue over the years, promote the right to a pension, to the fraudsters. The discovery of this scam allowed the Guardia di Finanza to save the sum of €881,925.50.

October 2010, Salerno

The investigations have allowed us to hypothesize the existence of a number of agricultural "ghost" holdings. Deception is to create a false company, declare the availability of land actually in use, make payments to third parties, and testified falsely to the INPS that farm workers have been hired, enabling the illegal distribution of agricultural unemployment, maternity, and disease benefits. At present, the survey involved more than seven hundred false workers, entrepreneurs, and professionals as well as the organizers of the scam. Given the complexity and prevalence of this phenomena, the investigation entrusted to the Centre of Tax Police are continuing and are aimed to establish the illegality of the contributions paid by INPS against several thousand farm laborers employed by companies operating in the district of Salerno.

Hear what he writes the weekly *Famiglia Cristiana,* on the Internet.

The final insult was discovered in the province of Salerno: 53 fictitious companies, 16,000 bogus employment relationships, and damages to INPS totalling €60 million. Scams were sometimes grotesque, with women workers in "motherhood" for eighty years. "But what emerges as a result of the INPS checks and the investigations of the police is just the tip of the iceberg," confirms Mr. Francis Sparagna, Director of the Department of Central Vigilance on revenue and economy of INPS.

How many fake agricultural workers there are, no one knows exactly. The Pension Fund has discovered 120,000 fictitious reports in 2006 alone. "The phenomenon is most impressive and is intertwined with organized crime."

On the evening of 23 November 1980, a violent earthquake hit Irpinia, in the regions of Campania and Basilicata, leaving nearly 3,000 dead and 280,000 homeless. In addition to this great tragedy suffered by the people, in the months and years to come, this earthquake had many nicknames: Irpiniagate, Terremotopoli, and Earthquake Infinity, for the many scandals of fraud committed by so many people against the state. Just think for a first estimate of costs for the reconstruction of 8,000 billion lire in 1981, he arrived at a total cost, without having solved the whole problem, of €66 billion in 2010.

In 1992, a year that will be famous in Italy for the start of the various powers of attorney, the investigation of the whole country, began the investigation "Hands on the earthquake" will be involved 87 people including the Hon. Ciriaco de Mita, the Hon. Paolo Cirino Pomicino, Senator Salverino De Vito, the Hon. Vincenzo Scotti, the Hon. Antonio Gava, the Hon. Antonio Fantini, the Hon. Francesco De Lorenzo, the Hon. Giulio Di Donato, and Commissioner Giuseppe Zamberletti. As to the involvement of politicians and administrators, complaints have been raised, prompting investigations that led to several arrests. It makes sense that if local politicians take possession of public monies in various ways, the people of the area will do the same. Indeed, the districts devastated by the first survey carried out, when it was time to receive public funds, increased dramatically. It was a dishonorable thing; it has enabled the people to manage public money. In a newspaper article, Sergio Rizzo described the difference between the reconstruction following the earthquake of May 1976 in Friuli-Venezia-Giulia and the one of November 1980 in Irpinia, between the regions of Campania and Basilicata.

He describes how twenty years after the earthquake in Friuli, everything gradually became just as it was before, as if nothing had happened, while in Campania in the south, after thirty years there were still areas affected by the earthquake that need to be fixed.

I suppose Rizzo and his fellow journalists should be thankful for the South, for if everything ran as it did in the North, there would be no public scandals to report to and therefore little for them to write about. Honesty doesn't make for good headlines, as does the dishonesty of the citizens of the Campania region.

When the Guardia di Finanza performed checks to see who had received the funds to rebuild factories, it found that many entrepreneurs had failed several times to make money, and once they did they disappeared. As always in the south, dishonesty is the norm. The police also discovered a rise in mega villas with swimming pools, where there was an old house with the stable. Many whose houses were not damaged by the earthquake received funds as well, and they simply tore down their old houses to build new ones. Entire villages behaved dishonestly, and when the reporter asked the mayor about the reason for such behavior, he responded simply, "What do you want that to be sued for wrongful death, by people who need it?" Was he suggesting it was their right, being close to the earthquake zone, to take advantage of the situation? However, what can you do in such a situation; put everyone in an entire county in priso

This reminds me of the book by Giorgio Bocca, which tells of a magistrate in Naples. He had made friends with this judge, who one day told him that was absent from the city, to go for control of illegal houses that were built in a neighboring village. "I take this opportunity to go home for a while," Bocca said to the magistrate. On my return to Naples, Bocca wrote in the book, I asked the magistrate as he went into the village, with the controls and how many houses demolished. Not one answered the magistrate; what he wants Mr Bocca, who tears down the whole village? There is even abusive police station, said the magistrate.

You see, things like this do not occur in the North. People with this mindset will damage the people of the north, importing their way of being and acting. When we move to another country, normally you adapt to the lifestyle of the place, but unfortunately too many Southerners, do not accept change, because they are too proud of their culture and their way of being, and this increases the discrimination against them.

Too many people do not like the southerners for this character, and anti-racist movements should try to understand why discrimination was established between the various ethnic groups. The question is very simple: because I've never heard to speak ill of Polish citizens, Bulgarians, Czechs, while there is discrimination against southern citizens.

Chapter 12

Puglia

January 2011: The Minister of Health, Fazio, since inspectors to investigate suspicious deaths in hospital in Bari, in the department of neurosurgery. We must thank, in addition to the families of the victims of medical malpractice, two anesthetists and a doctor who made the complaint (luckily there are still some good people who work in hospitals. Some people have been operated by the surgeon several times for the same cancer. Other times the patient is operated a second time so that the hospital(public or private does not matter) can collect more money from the State.

In their complaint, the two anesthetists described people remaining in hospital too long before surgery, and, very often, when they did receive their care, complications arose after surgery. Or patients with serious health problems did not receive the proper care.

Combing the Internet, I read some blogs about it, and I discovered that local officials did nothing except affirm my statements throughout this book.

Below is a letter from Mary, who accuses the hospital of having killed her son. Her son died in hospital in Bari, while another patient with the same condition who was operated on at the Gaslini Institute of Genoa is still alive.

Hear what he says Franco: "Go and heal in the centers of excellence, which are far from Bari. The University of Bari is in the hands of incompetent barons, old and tired, and their godchildren, with severe learning disabilities, who are researchers or 'associated' with competitions rigged by their godfathers."

Another person accuses the prosecutor of the republic of Bari of indifference. He calls upon the prosecutor to make the rounds of the wards, so he can see just how disastrous the situation is and how patients are neglected. If medical malpractice has been allowed to prosper for decades, it is the fault of the politicians, police, *"carabinieri"*, financial police, judiciary system, and finally the people. Everyone is responsible.

I would like to respond one the person, who goes by the handle "wake up Italy", who wrote a beautiful letter claiming that there are no hospitals in the Veneto region like the unfortunate hospital in Bari. In his correspondence he says that the hospital has benefited doctors, nurses, managers, and all those who work there, but certainly not the people who are being cared for. He says that doctors receive private visitations during working hours in the hospital, pocketing the fee. He neglects to declare that such transactions take place under the table, involving no taxes. However, it is only by making such black market payments that you will receive the proper care. See, Mr. wake up Italy, what happens in your part of the country, Puglia. You're not all like that—it is true—but what still happens in the south to this day scares me, and I, as a normal person, must strongly oppose the invasion of my country by people with such culture. It is the duty of every person to think of the good of their people.

In November 2010 the following headline appeared in the newspaper: "BARI. Buy judgments. Taxation and corrupt judges: 17 arrests". The article explained that 98 per cent of companies brought before the country's revenue agency who challenged their fees won their case. In fact, these companies paid bribes to judges to win these cases. Several people were arrested, including judges, lawyers, entrepreneurs, and officials of the regional tax commission. The damage to the treasury totaled €100 million.

In February 2011, the prosecutor in Bari asked for the arrest of senator of the Democratic Party, Alberto Tedesco, a former councilor of health of the region of Puglia. There was also an investigation into the management of health surveys in Puglia. The request must stop now be evaluated by the board for permission to proceed with the Senate. The charges included bribery, corruption, and fraud. The cases involved physicians, directors of local social and health units, and businessmen accused of receiving contracts from health Pugliese without competition.

Nichi Vendola, president of the Left, Ecology, and Freedom, governor of the Puglia region since 2005, defeated Raphael Fitto of the centre-right by a few votes. This good man, after four years governing the region, thanks to the numerous arrests made by police, realized there was great corruption in Puglia's health industry. Disconcert for the governor to the scandal that surrounds the centre-left politicians in the region for numerous arrests, in fact, asked and obtained that all councillors resign.

Vendola asked for help to the leaders of the political party UDC Pier Ferdinando Casini, offering important positions in the region of Puglia to the politicians of his party. Casini refused saying that his party will take the responsibility alone, in a year's time, when there will be elections.

Even the leader of the party Italia dei Valori (Italy of Values) Antonio Di Pietro refused his help to Vendola to form the new regional council, claiming that the elections were close, and he noticed that there was extensive corruption in the health of Puglia.

In an interview, Vendola admits that unfortunately in the Puglia, the interests of unscrupulous businessmen and corporations have continued to contribute to a costly and inefficient public health, where corruption reign supreme. Do not forget that the same Vendola began administrative investigations and informed the court of wrongdoing. Admittedly, Vendola has gained my confidence as a person and

116

politician. Unfortunately, it took me years to reach that conclusion as well. Vendola was re-elected governor for the centre-left in 2010.

March 2011: Foggia City

The police arrested businessman Vincent Nuzziello, Foggia ASL, two officials, and a professional installer on charges of corruption, including bid rigging. The military ascertained that Nuzziello, together with officials, and Nazario Granatiero Raffaele Di Stefano, put out an urgent tender for the purchase of tools for the operating rooms of hospitals in Cerignola, Foggia, Manfredonia, and San Severo, as their equipment had been stolen. In fact, not only had the equipment not been stolen, but there was no need to purchase additional medical equipment at a cost of €208,000.

At the home of Vincent Nuzziello, investigators found acts of the notice, along with the offerings of other companies involved in the bid. Five companies (CSS Foggia, Medical Shuttle, Genko Italy, The Medical, and Effe for Multiutility of Urbino), all indirectly controlled by Nuzziello, managed to win the races, thanks to the acts in his possession. The company that was awarded the contract, CSS, in three years had issued a single invoice and had no staff, had its registered office in via Greece 38, in the study of Nuzziello Anna (sister of Vincent), but at the moment Regional Councillor is not investigated.

After the purchase of unnecessary needles, even tools were not used and were found abandoned by NAS (Nuclei Antisofisticazioni e Sanità dei Carabinieri—Nucleus of Healt and against Adulteration of the Carabinieri).

Furthermore, the tools did not even work because they had not been tested. Nuzziello was placed under house arrest Granatiero Raphael, former director of the Heritage ASL, Nazario Di Stefano, employed in 'area management of the hospital of San Severo (which already hung conviction by a court for robbery, theft and property crime), which also did not create the titles for tenders, and John Bruno, contractor and installer.

In this scam which has cost 208,000 euros to the Region of Puglia, are involvedalso the entrepreneur Vincent Nuzziello and regional councilor Anna Nuzziello(sister of the entrepreneur).

Despite the scandals of corruption and embezzlement that occurred only a few years earlier, in 2011 the story continued unabated, as if people down there have no fear of going to jail. Even if we were inclined to put them in jail, what would we do as a society if it turned out we had to incarcerate 3 or 4 million people in the South? How much would that cost? This is not a joke. This is reality.

Bari

From an investigation began by the Guardia di Finanza in 2006, including wiretaps and video surveillance, a fraud was discovered involving the State University of Bari, in which thirty students tried to cheat to admissions, which allows only a limited number of medicine and dentistry students each year.

The University of Bari is home to the largest group of employees coming from the same family in all of Italy. This must be so, because this sort of anomaly in the north would cause all hell to break loose. Nine brothers and cousins, then there is the Pool family, with husband, wife, son and daughter, all hospital employees. This is the classic mindset of the people of the South: power is meant to be abused. A doctor who works in a hospital feels he is the master of the hospital. If you want to see a Mafia university, just go to the University of Bari, where a few families have taken possession of all the professorships. It has no equal in all of Europe.

In a university so dishonest and immoral, where a few clans have taken possession of all the chairs, it is only logical to expect rigged competitions, graduation exams sold for thousands of Euros, and other various atrocities. Naturally, those who did not have thousands of Euros to pay off university officials reported these practices to the judiciary. The scandal began in 2005, when the Guardia di Finanza realized that children, in-laws, and cousins of professors had overtaken the departments of Psychiatry, Neurosurgery, Orthopaedics, etc. The same surnames kept coming up in every department, providing irrefutable evidence that led Finance to assume control of all competitions and doctoral examinations.

Fraud in the Field

In spite of extensive TV coverage of scams involving the government body INPS (National Social Security Institute), nothing has been done to eliminate them, why?

Officials have discovered 120,000 false employment relationships but this is only the tip of the iceberg in the South, where this is a widespread phenomenon, with the help of trade unions and employers. The most egregious offense discovered by the Guardia di Finanza in Puglia was a peasant "mother" eighty years of age.

Dozens of farmers in the big phony roam Tavoliere or the Sele plain, recruiting thousands of labourers on paper in a well organized fraud against the state.

The final insult was discovered in the province of Salerno: 53 fictitious companies, 16,000 bogus employment relationships, and damages to INPS totalling €60 million. How many fake agricultural workers there are, no one knows exactly. The Pension Fund discovered 120,000 fictitious reports in 2006 alone. The phenomenon is most impressive and is intertwined with organized crime.

At each step of the Guardia di Finanza and *carabinieri* jump out from all sides: two or three thousand people, all people living on social welfare obtained by false papers. "They are 'farmers' who do not even have the land," says Colonel Antonio Tummillo of the Guardia di Finanza, office manager of Regional Command operations in Puglia. "They falsify everything from leases to other documents."

Since the scammers, once caught, show no assets, INPS is never able to recover the swindled funds, and the process in Italy takes so long that money obtained by fraud is almost never recovered. Then the same people find somewhere else in the region to continue the scam. For decades the race between cheaters and police has continued, with no solution to the problem. Since the 70s this shell game has continued in the South, thanks to popular custom as well as the complicity of various government agencies, and it is now impossible to defeat.

True, in recent years police control has intensified, but a civil society with such a bad habit is hard to beat without considering the huge social cost of controlling such people. In addition to the enormous amount of money stolen, these scams require considerable funds to keep under control. In agriculture, cheat, cheat with false contracts in public hospitals, by charging the services or things necessary, 3 or 4 times more. In public procurement, in order to pave roads, build bridges, or do anything else, prices are exorbitant due to the constant need to bribe politicians, payoff the Mafia, or whatever. It is a disaster so terrible that a normal can scarcely believe it. And yet to draw attention to this invites accusations of racism. I understand such accusations when they are leveled at me, but when anyone with a sense of humanity and justice examines all the details contained in this book, he will become more racist than I am, because they will not tolerate dealing with people from such a culture.

Near Foggia, a band of four people, including an INPS official, managed to draw 13 million into the coffers of our Pension Fund. They were discovered, 3700 false labourers, with a fake job, more than 50 days of work were entitled to unemployment benefits. With these false documents, false workers were entitled to all benefits offered by the INPS to legitimate workers.

Of fake farm labourers, 99 per cent are concentrated in five regions of the south, the first of which is Campania. Puglia wins the second spot with 1 false farmhand for every 157 inhabitants. These are followed by Sicily, Calabria, and Basilicata. The national average for fraud is 1 per every 600 inhabitants, and if we eliminated the five regions of the south, the number would be 1 false farmhand for every 49,000 inhabitants. Not to bad without the south, is it?

About Car Insurance

Premiums have increased 25 per cent, according to the monthly *Four Wheels*. The National Association of Insurance Companies indicates that the highest incidence of insurance fraud is in the Puglia region, with the mechanism of accidents bluff. Auto insurance is a paradise for cheaters and hell for honest motorists who have to pay large increases to cover for this fraud. Poor honest motorists in the Puglia region, you are right to complain against insurance companies, who make you pay for the sins of these cheaters.

Insurance companies were the first to implement Federalism, as it is hoped for by the League, throughout the country. In Naples, if you want car insurance against theft and fire, it is worth €20,000, because theft of insured cars is so commonplace in the South. Therefore, honest motorists must pay disproportionate increases as well, and it is only logical that their anger will soon make them feel justified in cheating the system themselves. Only severe penalties could put an end to these types of scams. The lenient policies of the past, implemented by all levels of government, have led to disaster. Even now in northern Italy there are foreign and southern circulating with false insurance coupons affixed to the glass of the car.

There are also people of the north displaying false tickets on their windshields, hoping that nothing will happen, but I think among many pirates of the road, there are those who run away because they do not have real insurance.

Pay Taxes? Are You Crazy?

2010 November

In the city of Bari, some employers as a result of tax audit of the Financial Police, were sanctioned for serious administrative irregularities, accounting for thousands if not millions of Euros in some cases. They had recourse to the Commission of the Province of Bari and the Puglia Regional Police through their intermediaries (accountants and lawyers) in the belief that they can illegally avoid or reduce the payment due in part to the Exchequer. The decision was that they had bestowed "gifts" to the tax courts and their officers, who were arrested or placed under investigation. The soldiers of the Guardia di Finanza found that at least eleven companies made use of this corrupt system, enacted by the Tax Commission of Bari.

The absurdity of what was happening the Tax Commission was that it was the judges, along with other officials, who were creating practices to earn money. These include judges looking for million dollar practice is, or those in which the businessman had to pay to the Exchequer a few million Euros. The corrupt judges in question negotiated with lawyers and accountants on the sum to be paid in exchange for a nice bit of money for them.

Only towards the end of the month of November did the Financial Police go into action, arresting seventeen people, including a judge, accountants, an official of the Tax Commission, and a group of businessmen and bankers. Who knows how long this scam went on and how many hundreds of millions of Euros went missing from the coffers of the state over the last thirty to forty years. If this is embedded in the culture, what can you do to stop it? And if this was discovered in a single city in the South, how many other cities with criminal groups, such as Naples, in the Campania region, was this happening in? How many billions of Euros in recent decades have not been paid throughout the south? And those who did do such enormous damage to the country found it easy to remain under house arrest, extend the process time, and then drop them in the prescription. But what are we to do, put a few million people in prison? In southern Italy are trying to stop, stopping every now and then, in the same place in the judicial corruption, fraud to the state, is continued by others. This is part of the culture, and in a Catholic country like Italy, the extreme measures needed to stop it are too unpopular and will never be implemented, thus leaving the country in the hands of criminals.

A *Panorama* reporter infiltrated the hospital wards of Isernia (Molise region) dressed as a doctor to demonstrate the degradation that prevailed in the ward. After two months he described in an article everything that had been going on in the hospital. The person who encouraged the journalist to take up the investigation was fired. This person, a doctor, defended himself by saying he knew nothing of the false doctor, but it was useless. However, the people paid to do the cleaning but left the place filthy, or those caught on film smoking in the halls in the corridors of the hospital, saw no action taken against them. In short, the hospital employees can do what they want, without respect for the sick, as long it what goes on inside the hospital is never revealed to the outside world.

Definitely, seeing doctors failing to don masks and gloves before surgery was a shocking testimony to the total lack of respect towards patients.

Chapter 13

North Colonized by Mafia from the South and Its Damage

Mafia is a term used to describe gangs all over the world. However, in this chapter we will discuss the Italian Mafia of southern origin.

These criminal organizations are born in places where it is easier to aggregate the people for different causes, such as poverty, laziness, lack of desire to work, or pursuit of personal wealth. There are three big criminal organizations in Italy: the Mafia in Sicily, the Camorra in Campania, and the 'Ndrangheta in Calabria. In Northern Italy, on the other hand, no such organizations existed, because the culture is too different. From the 60s onwards, these organizations were strengthened with earnings from drugs and extortion. Then they began to invade the northern regions of Tuscany, Liguria, Piedmont, Valle d'Aosta, and Lombardy.

Justice: Too many southern prisoners? Federal prison
From the newspaper Il Giornale, 7 January 2009
This newspaper is widespread nationally, and one of the best in my opinion.

According to the Ministry of Justice, on 30 June 2009, there were 63,630 being held in the country's prisons for various reasons. To release information on the places of birth of these inmates is not politically correct, but it is significant. "Natives" (total population 39,389) are in jail at a rate of 0.68 people per thousand inhabitants, or 1 for every 1,463 Italian citizens. On the other hand, foreigners (total prison population 24,241) are incarcerated at a rate of 6.21 per thousand, or 1 in every 161 people. However, this number may be distorted, because we can only estimate the number of total immigrants in the country, as many are here illegally. In any case, the ratio is disturbing. It is even more interesting to analyze national origins. At the time of the survey there were 8,741 European inmates (including 4,525 non-EU). Ranking prisoners by percentage, there are 30 Tunisians, 25 Nigerians, 13 Moroccans, and "only" 6 Albanians in prison for every thousand immigrants. The Chinese, though, one of the largest communities (170,265 regular immigrants), are virtually absent from the charts, because they are on their way, trying to show himself as little as possible: however, the suspicion arises that, aside that health care facilities and commercial, including a judicial system of their own. The Gypsies disappear into the folds of the statistics, as they come here under various nationalities that do not allow a consolidation of data, which might be rather enlightening.

Without foreign immigration, there would be 38.1 per cent fewer prisoners; given the astronomical cost of keeping them, that would be quite a savings. The data on inmates do not have a direct connection with that of crime, because convicted criminals often commit more than one criminal act; also, 74 per cent of crimes go unpunished and a further number are not even reported, but it is legitimate to think that in the absence of foreign immigrants, crime would decrease at least the same percentage, and whereas most foreigners can easily escape the controls (even more so if they are illegal) and that are dedicated primarily to those very types of crimes that are reported less.

The ministry statistics also include the regional origin of indigenous prisoners and allow for other interesting considerations. Even among the Italians there are significant differences: the highest percentage of inmates are those born in the Campania region (1.86 per thousand, and one per 538 inhabitants). Next are those from Sicily (1.53 and 653), then Calabria (1.50 and 665) which was close to the data of Asian immigrants and exceeded the percentages of several ethnic groups considered individually. The most virtuous are the regions of Valle d'Aosta (one per 8,570 inhabitants a recluse), then Umbria (7855), Marche (6328), and Emilia (one for every 5,577 inhabitants).

Only 11.23 per cent of all convicts were born in the Po-alpine regions, which, taken together, have 0.27 inmates per thousand inhabitants and 1 convict per 3,588 people. Data from the rest of Italy are respectively 1.01 and 992, only those of the former territory of the Kingdom of the Two Sicilies 1.4 and 701.

Considering all the prisoners, domestic and foreign, Italy is in the top twenty countries of the Council of Europe, at thirteen places, in inmates per population. With no foreigners they would jump to fifth place, after Slovenia, Finland, Denmark, and Malta. This fact should make you think a lot about chanting the mantra immigrants are always a positive resource.

Pushing forward the same simple but effective reasoning that has been done on the state of law in the absence of immigrants, escaping also to consider that in a state of genuine autonomy and strict control of imported crime, Padania would be easy to a great deal of offense in less than 75 per cent and be the safest country in Europe. This is a good reason to start thinking seriously about the project of "judicial federalism".

The statistics shows that only 11.23 per cent of prisoners in the north, excluding the region of Emilia-Romagna, well, with our culture of order and discipline, it could further reduce this figure, because the crime would not learn as it is unfortunately now, and would not have many drug addicts in jail, because for us in the north, the drug addict should be treated, not left alone, abandoned to itself as it is now. Too often killings are committed, both at home and outside the family, by drug addicts, because not enough is being done to counter the drug trade and because we do not act firmly when it comes to helping drug addicts. However, the data, reported in not only one but all the serious newspapers, speaks for itself.

As a result, please allow the people of Veneto to hold a referendum to regain their freedom of choice. Venetian citizens need autonomy so we may pursue our way of life. It must not come from Rome, with its stupid, vile, corrupt laws. Southerners, this is nothing to be angry about. Venetian wish to govern themselves due to the simple fact that Italy has not worked well together; indeed, that Venetians have been subjected to these laws has damaged everyone. Now the Venetian must get by on his own.

The Wicked Behavior of the Southern People

Now there are too many years I've heard of "Southern Question" in Italy.

I always hear problems about it for years, without any resolve. I'm disgusted just hear those two words.

The people of the South are so proud that I have become accustomed to hearing their claims. According to them, all their misfortunes are the fault of North, the Piedmontese, who invaded their territory in 1860 with the scoundrel Garibaldi. Even we in the North curse Garibaldi, who foisted this unwanted "national unity" upon us. We in the North are tired of your way of approaching life, living by your wits, cheating the Italian state and private insurance whenever possible. It is true that not all Southerners are so bad, but when a citizen of North reads that his per capita income could be equivalent to that in Germany, but knows he must lose 30 to 40 per cent of his income in taxes, he must conclude that something is not right. When a citizen of the north continues to hear national news stories about false workers discovered in the south who cheat the National Insurance Institute (INPS), pointing to its knees security status, and that 99 per cent of fraud is carried out in southern Italy, we cannot remain silent for fear of being called racist.

I have written this book to describe the events that occur in the South because it's time to stop these unrelenting claims that southerners are merely defending themselves against oppressors. When a person continues for decades to defraud anyone, that person cannot be defended to the bitter end. You can defend one who has nothing and steals from hunger, I agree, because it is unacceptable for a person to suffer from hunger. But when hundreds of thousands of citizens in southern Italy continue to perpetrate scams, no normal person can find this defensible.

The so-called southern problem will never succeed, at least in the next few decades, to solve their problems because it is nothing, that the expression of a people, its culture and way of life, totally different from the peoples of the north. When the Wall fell in Berlin, West Germany, despite East Germany's miserable history of communism, she managed to develop and progress. After little more than twenty years, the former East German people have a better standard of living than in the southern Italian regions of Calabria, Campania, Sicily, Puglia, and Basilicata. Why, despite their advantages, do southern Italians continue to live by 1960s standards, while East Germany has achieved a good standard of living? The difference is the culture of the two peoples, because two separate Germanies, when combined, comprised a similar people with the same culture, but while unfortunately the South of Italy is composed of people with an abysmally different culture compared to the people of the North.

The differences from the late Roman Empire, which fell for the Negroid populations with repeated mastication imported as slaves.

After the collapse of the 'Roman Empire across the peninsula was, fortunately for us, invaded by barbarians famous, Germanic and Nordic.

Lombards, Normans, Goths, Suevi . . .

After the fall of Rome's Italy was invaded by the so-called barbarian peoples.

The "barbarians" saved the Germans' Italy, which has become a melting pot of races. So much so that Italy, even after the 'invasion' barbarians 'become' a world centre of culture and 'art, and still' a nation rich and culturally advanced. Greece and Egypt, although, as the 'Italy created great civilizations' and be collapsed for non-white immigration, did not suffer the' Germanic invasion, and today are poor and underdeveloped nations.

The north was occupied massively than in the south.

That's why the people of northern Italy is more similar to the peoples of Northern Europe, to the south are more similar to the Middle East.

Of course the development of a particular type of society depends on the population:

Nordic peoples have always advanced company created and developed

This is true even in Italy: As we move away from the zone of influence Nordic-Celtic we approach the Middle East.

Southerners may not like this interpretation, but it is largely confirmed by the facts. Europe should take note of this; when dealing with any Southerner he casts himself as the victim. They claim that they have been exploited since 1860, when the Piedmontese government stole millions in the south, as they continue to say (on Wikipedia, it says that there is to ascertain that those who had gold coins, has received the 'equivalent in paper money by the government of the time), then I do not think that the Bourbons, they returned to Spain with empty coffers, via, let's be realistic.

Even the southerners who insist upon unification have encouraged gang activity in their country. Simply go on the Internet and look for the name Elizabeth Gaskell, who, before 1860, wrote a good book which explains the culture of the South, which continues to this day. It describes very well how the Camorra is involved in every sector of business, and how everyone had to pay protection money. The book, entitled *An Italian Institution*, refutes your claims that you are victims and shows how this behavior is bred right into your character. Southerners, read and learn how your ancestors were. This author wrote this book with no interest in creating falsehoods. Foreign writers more than 150 years ago were genuine and described what they saw without embellishment.

I invite all Southerners with access to the web to read the Wikipedia page "The Southern Question". Afterwards, think well upon your arguments. Keep in mind that Wikipedia is a serious organization and is not biased. Even in 1860 the North was more developed than the south, despite your prideful boasts to the contrary. In fact, there were vast differences prior to the unification of the two peoples into one state. Agriculture in the north was widespread due to sharecropping, which consisted of a contract between the owner of the land and the farmer, who worked the land, receiving half of what it produced. In this way it stimulated people to work harder and led to a robust agricultural industry. In the south there was land ownership (as in the Middle Ages), with many owners, including the church, owning vast uncultivated tracts of lands. In Lazio, there are still many wetlands, which are breeding grounds for malaria. Also, for large landowners living in the countryside there was no incentive to produce more. They were content merely to have a lot of land.

Meanwhile, in northern Italy in 1870, the standard of living for the people improved slightly when federalism replaced feudalism, whereas in the South it did not improve at all, as large landowners refused to invest their earnings. The common practise was to hoard cash so they could buy even more land. Only the Duce Benito Mussolini in the 20s managed to redistribute land to peasants.

In 1839 (twenty-one years prior to unification) the first railway was built in Italy in Naples. It was 8 km long. In 1860, the only Southern railway, in Naples, reached 100 km. Meanwhile, in the north, there were over 2,000 km of railway. And these were not built with the money of the south.

Another huge difference scene after the unification was in the general election. While in the north there was a bourgeois society composed of many social classes, in the south politicians represented large landowners, who, as I mentioned before, begin to disappear with the advent of fascism under Benito Mussolini.

During the First and Second World War, industries developed further in the north, which makes sense, as there were many industries in the North with skilled workers.

The south, on the other hand, did not have the ability to produce as the North did. Although the Kingdom of the Two Sicilies was the prize before the unification of Italy, afterwards industrialization stopped there, while in the North it continued to progress. The evidence is clear. Naples was the first city in Italy to have the km.7.25 long railway, built in 1839. In 1860 occurred the national unity, while in the north therewere 2,000 kilometers of railway, in the south, in Naples there were less than 100 km.

To which the people did not think at all, would not otherwise have served to control the people of the Camorra, as described in the book, the English traveler Gaskell. The evidence that such a union took place is available to all. Once held on the system fell by the Bourbons, with the Camorra, the Mafia and other criminal organizations that controlled the people, manifested the first directed against the Piedmontese army.

Wars cost money, and the social parasites in the south (i.e., the Mafia) did not accept the change. Riots ensued, and to quell the riots, 150,000 troops were sent to the south. To fight the southern bandits, a lot of money was spent. In short, the criminal mindset existed in southern Italy long before unification, and any allegations to the contrary are useless. I see that in my country, Veneto, there has never been an organization as powerful as those found in the south. Veneto was annexed thanks to a plebiscite fraud, and it has continued to suffer after the unification of Italy. The people of Veneto have not the courage of the peoples of the south. Yet the Venetian people do not complain; they work and produce, trying to improve their standard of living.

Let us now leave the distant past and examine what has happened in the last few decades, from the 60s onwards. Why, that was capable of becoming the Veneto, he could have also the region of Campania, Calabria, Sicily, etc., because even the southern regions, have been funding such as the Veneto, if not most of the Veneto.

You see, with modern communications, it is easy to be aware of everything that happens around us, and so we know what occurred in the South from the 50s onwards. Too many points out cultural diversity as the cause of poverty in the south. Giorgio Bocca wrote a book about it. So did journalists Gian Antonio Stella and Sergio Rizzo, whose book *Drift* explains very well who is to blame for this economic disaster. Then, if you go to read about the hospitals in the country, where do you find the worst ones located? Even in the south. Just read the book *The Fair of Health*, written by Daniela Minerva.

There is no doubt that corruption exists in the North. Unfortunately, the north of Italy has not been immune, as other European countries have, from the invasion of Mafia, Camorra, 'Ndrangheta, and especially those who fancy themselves more intelligent than others. In my research, I I have confirmed that the North has been infiltrated by southern leaders. The call massomafie I Appendsouth, which, with rigged contests, inserted themselves into key positions all the way from the top reaching down to even small towns, whose people, having the same culture, were easy to train. In the courts, now are all Southerners, not even counting the police, the Guardia di Finanza, or anyone else. One question remains in my mind. How come a few months ago, in a vegetable market of Verona, a shipment of cocaine (300 kg) was seized from the Russian Mafia? Yet it turns to drugs in Verona, however, you must seize the drugs of competition, not that of the 'Ndrangheta, you think? This is why the powerful Mafias, with the collusion of officials in the various competitions, so that they are to win then people will be easy to buy, if you do not buy before they win the competition.

The story speaks for itself, and there is no need to accuse anyone. There have been so many scandals involving the Italian secret services, which are either corrupt or in league with various criminal organizations in the south. Think about it: secret service men, paid for by taxes of the citizens, instead of serving the interests of those who pay, in this case the state, they think about their business with the lights. They involve themselves with the Mafia, with the Camorra, and with black extremists just to make money. And if we look at the employees of the services, it appears that nine out of ten are people from the south. Intelligence agencies have also been involved in the trafficking of radioactive and toxic waste and other crimes.

Now I ask you a simple thing. As a Venetian person who has become aware of this, should I accept that my country has been so shamelessly invaded by southern leaders? In Calabria, the leaders from the north, taken by the Regional Doris Lo Moro, were expelled because they were considered foreigners. For goodness' sake, they were right to hunt, because they were not the territory.

A few years ago, all the national newscasts gave prominence to a penitent 'Ndrangheta who confessed that many old ships carrying toxic waste were scuttled off the coast of Calabria in Cetraro. He spoke for a while, then you do not hear more talk, indeed, from the findings that there was no waste on board. However, the unification of Italy has encouraged the spread of crime from the south to the north. Then, in the 1970s, the Mafia carried out a number of terrible kidnappings, some ending with death. These abominable crimes were committed in large part by the Mafia and 'Ndrangheta. Even Berlusconi became afraid, and to defend himself, he took as a hedge of groom a Mafia Mangano in his villa in Arcore. One thing is certain, in Italy there were kidnappings quite abnormal. In 1978, Aldo Moro, the leader of the DC, was kidnapped and later killed, and a few years later, Cyril Cyrus from the DC's Campania was also kidnapped, until his political friends as Gava, through contacts with the Camorra, managed to free him.

The south of Italy, as well as foreign populations, is the largest provider of inmates of Italian prisons. Without the south and foreigners, the country's prisons would be nearly empty. Just think of the Campania region, whose various rackets give such a hard time to its institutions. In the Calabria region, the 'Ndrangheta controls all social life, public procurement, and hospitals, where patients are treated worse than animals. Then there is the Sicilian Mafia, which continues to control the social lives of Sicilians.

These three large criminal organizations, I must reiterate, became powerful because of the politicians of the south fifty years ago, who instead of fighting them at the beginning joined forces to gain votes. Many politicians gained personally, at the cost of enormous damage to local populations, and the result is what we see now: while the north has improved their standard of living, the south is lagging behind. On the other hand, were the people of forty to fifty years ago to join forces and become part of criminal organizations? It was not the Piedmontese army, right? Or do you wish to propagate the usual accusations against the Piedmontese army, which "ruined the south".

The damage that the people of the south did, not just to the north of the country but to all of Europe, has been devastating. When a territory has been invaded by an arrogant and wicked people, the people who live in the invaded territory have the right to rebel, and I rebelled, and this book will reveal your arrogance to the world so that you can be driven back home. Often I think of all those people from the 50s onwards who suffered believe at the hands of criminal clans from the south. In the 60 and 70 thousands penetrated northern labour regions. Imagine, those of you reading this book, having a bar, a shop, or a restaurant, and one day having two or three men come in and ask you to pay protection money. If you refuse they will beat you, and if you refuse them further or report them to the police, someone will burn your car or destroy your bar or shop. I never had these problems, but believe me, but there are plenty of stories from those who have. And in southern Italy, the criminals are so numerous. It's easy to talk about racism, but when a peaceful people are humiliated, we cannot pretend that no one is angry about it.

April 2011: The hands of the Cosa Nostra, the waste of the north

Seized assets for 22 million Euros related to the boss Luigi Palermo Abbate: with his company managed numerous contracts in Lombardy and Liguria.

The company would win tenders by threatening competitors and even officials with violence, which was induced to reveal information covered by professional secrecy. Aside from Italy 90, police seized another company due to newly created Abbate, the "Environment Ecoitalia Ltd.", located in Palermo, the bigger the activity of recycling, processing, and disposal of municipal solid waste.

Both owners, Maria Abbate, Demma and Claudio, were arrested in 2009 on the orders of the prosecutor of Lodi for bid rigging, bribery and illegal disposal of waste.

September 2008: Police discovered a number of hazardous materials, including thousands of tons of arsenic, zinc, lead, indium, germanium, and mercury from "Pertusola" instead of being disposed of in landfill were used in construction.

Schools, parks, roads, houses, and public works were constructed with these hazardous, carcinogenic materials. Also seized in Operation Black Mountains was at least eighteen areas scattered throughout the territory, up to Cutro Crotone and Capo Rizzuto, high-density areas in the hinterland Mafia. The prosecution of Crotone, coordinated by deputy prosecutor Pierpaolo Bruni, took steps to seize the structures at the centre of the investigation. Seven people have been entered in the register of suspects. At least 350,000 tons of toxic materials have been used to build, among other things, three courtyards of a number of schools, including St. Francis Elementary and a technical institute, both of Croton, and an elementary school in Cutro. Arsenic, zinc, lead, indium, germanium, mercury, and other toxic substances from the wastes of special "Pertusola" Crotone, instead of being disposed of legally and with caution, were used in the construction. These materials should be treated in specialized landfills instead of being sold to construction companies, who used it in the building of houses, a wharf, and roads. The seven suspects include legal representatives of construction companies and company health officials:

- Vincent Hand, legal representative pro-tempore of Pertusola south, which shut down operations in the late 90s
- John Ciampi, legal representative of the business
- Paolo Girelli, legal representative of Bonatti
- Mungari Alfred, legal representative of Leto Construction
- Dominic Colosimo, Francis Curcio, and Dominic Ruscio Curcio, the three Regional Health Authority officials

All seven men were charged with conspiracy. The seizure of the eighteen areas was brought to the attention of the president of the province of Crotone, Sergio Iritale who released the following statement.

> The news—we read—confirmation, if it were needed, the exceptional seriousness of the environmental situation of large parts of the province and, in particular, the responsibility as the occurrence of this situation, have had policies of aggression to the territory and plunder of resources for many years carried out by Eni through its subsidiaries and activities conducted in the province of Crotone. This—the note continues—is the result of the logic of profit at all costs, he found the place blind and insensitive ruling classes. Even the areas of information, on the altar of petty economic interests, turned a blind eye to disturbing reality, which is now revealed in all their explosive negativity. Incalculable damage has been caused to human health, the environment, the production system.

Blood analysis performed on 290 students in an elementary school in San Francisco and a commercial technical institute Lucifer showed traces of cadmium, nickel, and arsenic. Suspicions were raised when many children started to get sick for reasons unexplained. These reasons, unfortunately, were connected to the illegal dumping of toxic waste: such as materials incorporated in the pillars of structures in

Salerno-Reggio Calabria, which were also used in the foundations of two schools and other public works.

Part of radioactive waste, presumably came from 'South Pertusola industry, known for its zinc processing, a material altament toxic.

September 2009: "We are afraid to leave our children in this school." These are the words of Joan, the mother a twelve-year-old boy, who today (14 September 2009) would begin school at the Alcmaeon Institute. There is nothing strange about this, except that the school in question is literally surrounded by toxic waste. The starting point is the overcrowding of the school conveyed by increase enrollments. Provided that the principal seems to have forced the institute to reopen classrooms of St. Francis School, which had its own toxic waste in the subsurface.

It jumps to the headlines of the investigation "Black Mountain" last September that has impounded several sites, "St. Francis" included. According to the prosecutor's office, because of Crotone, the school's basement contained a dangerous amount of toxic waste. However, the leadership of the institute and the council declared the site safe, since the waste had been covered with concrete.

Could mere cement safeguard the health of the students in that school? Perhaps this is true just in case you avoid working on this land. Certainly, the best solution would have been to dig up the entire site. Given that they did not, it is only natural that parents would be concerned.

Actual journeys of hope, in the locality of the north. The parents of many children in Croton tried to save all their children. Have poisoned them to him. They went to school every day, never thinking they were resting their feet on a huge carpet of radioactive waste, never suspecting they were breathing poison for several hours a day. Now many of them are suffering from cancer, and they need treatment. Substances including zinc, cadmium, and nickel have found in their stomach and hair. Keep their feet on the former slag Pertusola South, breathing the poisons of the former South Pertusola. They did this for ten years.

Yes, because the poisons of South Pertusola investigation was opened in 1998. For ten years, however, the dossier collected dust due to neglect. He thought the deputy prosecutor of Crotone, Pierpaolo Bruni, would open the Black Mountains investigation in 2008. According to estimates by Bruni, until 1996, at least 200,000 cubic yards of material were stored in warehouses of the company, equivalent to 400,000 tons of slag. "Black Mountains", black mountains. Black poison. The mayor of Croton, Peppino Vallone, is among the most active: some days ago he ordered the indefinite closure of St. Francis School and Lucifer Business Technical Institute. "We are forced to live in a city in which the 'Ndrangheta kills your children as they play soccer. Most people are not outraged," he told strill. It 21 September last year, has to deal with a city poisoned.

It is sad to hear that such inconceivable things could happen to another human being. People poison others for the sake of money, then accuse companies in the North. But was it the people of the North who built with toxic materials in Calabria? Or was it part of the Calabrian society? This is why I do not want managers that come from your land, even if it is true that there are many good people in Calabria. It is my right to demand that in my country there are local leaders, just as it is your right to do so in yours. Each man must be the master of his own home.

December 2003: On 6 November the prosecutor of Santa Maria Capua Vetere (Caserta), Donato Ceglie, made another attempt to open Operation Cassiopeia, issuing ninety-seven requests for trial for smuggling a million tons of hazardous waste. The serious charges included conspiracy, environmental disaster, poisoning of the waters, illegal dumping, fraud and abuse of office, which, thanks to the decriminalization of environmental crimes, has not led to a single arrest.

Note:

In southern Italy there is a saying; the toxic waste came from the rich north. Well I answer them by saying that, with their mafias they have destroyed, beyond belief, the rich North. And no person carries garbage to the south, if not criminal organizations from the south.

They made their way to the Mafia clans and clans of the Camorra, which then buried them in agricultural lands. These lands, as usual, were never identified. Expresses satisfaction with the operation, the Legambiente, which carries the 94 stops a battle against trafficking in toxic waste and sees engaged in Calabria a valuable young lawyer, Rudolf Ambrosio, to go up against to such traffic. The news of the indictments of 97 required for each of the huge traffic of waste from North to South—bodes well for Henry Fountain, environmental manager and legality of Legambiente. "That waste disposal and illegal dumping," explained Fountain, "is a huge wound to our country. And after the uproar of the case Enichem Priolo, Operation Cassiopeia, it insists there." Just think that every year, more than 11 million tons of waste has disappeared into thin air. This activity involved as many as twenty-two criminal clans, and that the market is around rubbish connection, only for special waste, around €2.6 billion. "Investigations like this," concludes Fountain, "demonstrate the increasing aggressiveness of the eco-Mafia."

Once again, we notice the southern culture, with their phrases like "opulent north". But Christ, God, who by unfair competition, as your countrymen is that traffic. How many factories would have been closed in the north because of unfair competition between criminal firms from the South? Have you ever asked? Southerners will never change; they will always be the victims. What about unfair competition on the procurement of small towns in the north, where to win the contracts because they are too bearish, they were almost always, construction firms from the south. This is what happened to the mayor of a village near mine, in Veneto, who refused to pay the full amount of a contract for a company from the south, because it had not paved a road in accordance with the contract. For a while, the mayor needed the accompaniment of a bodyguard, because he was being threatened by southerners. After while, he grew tired of spending money on the bodyguard and agreed to pay the company from the South. I'm sure he has learned from this experience.

A History of Toxic Waste That Could Be Stored

They are nineteen and are being investigated and charged for the disposal of toxic waste. Between 1995 and 1998, 35 thousand tons of waste from zinc ferrites from Pertusola industry of Crotone should be disposed of through a set of permissions obtained from the Calabria region, through the Regional Minister Sergio Stanco. However, these ferrites never reached the plant site in Sardinia and were instead buried in the soils of Cassano Ionian and Sybaris. The process was only the beginning for all the defendants, who had been divided into two through bureaucratic tricks. One group, involving the crime of corruption, was in the hands of the judges of Castrovillari, while the other was brought up for environmental disaster in the courts of Catanzaro. Six hearings followed the indictment in Castrovillari, but in Catanzaro, where there were seven hearings, no trial was held. After seven and a half years nineteen people were implicated in illegal trafficking of toxic waste in Calabria in various capacities, waiting to be judged.

December 2010: In the village of Brescello, in communist Emilia-Romagna, there was a brave woman, Catia Silva, secretary of the Lega Nord party. This woman denounced the infiltration of 'Ndrangheta in public procurement. For ten years she denounced it, but politicians from the left did not listen; in fact, they said she would never win the election. But this woman continued to remain interested in the truth, not in tricks that criminals use to win contracts, followed by poor execution of their work. Men of the clan have repeatedly threatened her, but she is not afraid, perhaps because she is the child of a policeman. Even other people in the League in that region were threatened.

Allow me to present you some headlines from 2011 just to give you an idea of how efficient organized crime from the south is.

'Ndrangheta in Lombardy: 35 arrests and seized assets

The operation coordinated by Ilda Boccassini. The arrested suspects including illegal disposal of waste and drug dealing. Anti-Mafia" 'Ndrangheta colonize the north."

'Ndrangheta/Goods for 1,600 million euros seized by Dia

Reggio Calabria, 11 November (TMNews)—Operation of the Dia (Anti-Mafia Investigation Department) of Reggio Calabria, this morning. The officers of Colonel Ardizzone have placed i.

'Ndrangheta/Croton, seized assets of 4 million euros

Catanzaro, 3 November (TMNews)—Assets held for four million have been seized in a joint operation this morning to Maesano of Isola Capo Rizzuto clan in the province of . . . larena. it | 15 days ago

Seized movable and immovable property worth two million euros to affiliate to an alleged 'Ndrangheta

Seals of movable and immovable property worth two million euros. The operation conducted by police involved an alleged affiliated with the 'Ndrangheta, BriguoriAugustine, accused . . . nanopress. it | 197 days ago

'Ndrangheta: Operation "Reggio South"—33 arrests and seized 60 million of assets. And 'the third operation against' ndrine in 4 days

Reggio Calabria—The last in order of time is the operation "Reggio South." 33arrests, seized goods to the value of 60 million euros, including 21 companies, 6soils with numerous buildings and real estate. Within four days is the third big operation against the Calabrian 'ndrine. 105 arrests, . . . calabrianotizie. | 252 days ago

Operation against the 'Ndrangheta in Lombardy: 35 arrests, seized assets to 2 million

New blow to the 'Ndrangheta rooted in the north. Thirty-five arrests against membersof many Calabrian criminal organization are ongoing at this time by the nucleus of the Guardia di Finanza tax police in Milan, the ROS Carabinieri, in collaboration with the Police . . .

ilfattoquotidiano. it | 249 days agoInizio modulo

Blitz against the 'Ndrangheta: 300 arrests. More recent major operation . . .

Maxiblitz of policemen and police against the 'Ndrangheta: more than 300 people arrested. The deal, the largest . . .

'Ndrangheta, 8 arrests. "Masters in the yards"—ViviMilano

after four years of investigations, the Guardia di Finanza in Milan dismantles a group ('ndrina) tied to one of the most important clans of the' Ndrangheta in the north. Eight arrests . . .

milano.corriere.it/cronache/articoli/2008/07_Luglio/11/arresti_ndrangheta.shtml

'Ndrangheta, ten arrests in Reggino

Eight people have ended up in handcuffs at dawn today in the context of the operation "Robin. He is accused of having favoured the inaction of Gregory and Joseph Bellocco of . . .

'Ndrangheta, hit two gangs of Locri, 27 arrests . . . Two clans of the 'Ndrangheta of Locri who extort the traders . . . Other Items

'Ndrangheta: 20 arrested in Lombardy—Tgcom-record—page 1

The State Police of Lecco, at the conclusion of a survey conducted in collaboration with the Flying Squad and the Guardia di Finanza in Milan, has executed 20 orders . . .

Anti-Blitz'Ndrangheta, 300 arrests

One hundred and twenty latches arranged by the DDA in Reggio Calabria, 180 arrests . . . were organic to the 'Ndrangheta and the point of being . . . RECENT ARTICLES

Calabria, 40 arrests' Ndrangheta, also the mayor and councilors

Locri, Reggio Calabria (Reuters)—The Flying Squad of Reggio Calabria has arrested 40 people today, including the mayor and some aldermen of a seaside resort, accused . . . it.reuters

Voice—'Ndrangheta, 6 arrests for the clans of Gioiosa Jonica

Related articles: • 'Ndrangheta, a big blitz in Locri: • 11 arrests' Ndrangheta, 50arrests in the works . . . 'Ndrangheta, 6 arrests for clans di Gioiosa Jonica Stop the authors of

November 2011 Reggio Calabria

In handcuffs the Reggio well, acted as nominee in the affairs of gangs

'Ndrangheta, controlled the company' of the City, 11 arrests

Blow to the gang-Tegano De Stefano

Note:

But you know, all these criminals from the south, how much they cost to the Italian government? In the north, we will have 10% of detainees without foreigners and southerners.

Professionals, entrepreneurs, lawyers, and people close to the secret service and the Masons: all at the service of the 'Ndrangheta, willing to act as nominee or help in business. Heavy charges that led to eleven orders of preventive detention and the seizure of €50 million from people close to the powerful clans Tegano De-Stefanogli.

To complete the operation of 150 financiers GICO Core Tax Police of Reggio Calabria, at the request of the District Anti-Mafia Directorate of Reggio Calabria. The financiers are doing numerous searches, some of which were in professional, commercial and legal.

An arrest warrant was also issued for John Tegano, head of the gang already in prison. Among those affected by the measure was mole Young Zumbo, who was tied to intelligence services and provided information on the transactions in advance to the gangs, his wife, Mary Frances Toscano, a lawyer, his sister Patricia Zumbo, and her brother Robert, who is an Emo accountant.

They are affected by the measure also the entrepreneur Joseph Rechichi, who had held administrative positions in the municipal Multiservizi. Other nominees and supporters of the clan included the brother of the entrepreneur and his two sons.

According to investigators with the favors of these fine exponents of Reggio Calabria, which also involved relatives and friends, the 'Ndrangheta was able to control a part of the private capital of the Municipality of Reggio Calabria municipal Multiservice SPA. It was in the hands of the gang Recim Ltd., which controls 33 per cent of the companies' territorial management services Ltd., which in turn controls 49 per cent of the Multiservice Srl. Discovered in the survey a large portion of the so-called "gray area", and the one that 'made up of professionals in the service of the thighs

Just read what is happening in the city of Reggio, Calabria, to understand how the most important civil positions in that society, such as police chief, finance chiefs, magistrates, and teachers in public schools were deeply involved with criminals. Not to mention lawyers, intelligence officers, and politicians. I still cannot figure out how people in my country can tolerate Southerners occupying these positions. For goodness' sake, there are good people in the South—there is no doubt about it—but I cannot pretend that in my country these positions should not be occupied by Venetians. Is that too much to ask? If I am racist for asking it because this is supposedly a multiethnic society, then I am proud to be called a racist. What matters is that in Veneto, the culture of Veneto survives. Otherwise, we will be left with the culture of Gypsies.

From the site interner "LIBRE association of ideas"
July 2010
Asbestos, Ontario poisoned to death by the 'Ndrangheta
Posted on 16/7/10 in • Category: Reports

For those of Calabria is like reinventing the wheel," says Joseph Baldessarro, one who writes about 'ndrina for 15 years for running illegal dumpsites in Calabria and explores sunken ships laden with nuclear waste. Discover, as it is written in the order of the investigating magistrate in Milan against the new network of Calabrian Mafia families in Lombardy, one of the companies controlled by the 'ndrina, "PeregoRoads," in his yard smaltisse toxic waste, primarily asbestos, will not budge that much. Author of the book "Poisoned" with Manuela IATI—where we talk about waste of nuclear power plants and electric, container and industrial waste dioxin in Seveso—says they are trifles compared to the rubbish with which they have sunk nuclearCalabria, those residues of asbestos scattered between the lakes and the Lomellina.

"Asbestos? In Calabria there are tons every summer on the beaches, from one to another province, taken years ago by some kind of factories of the industrialized North, "Claudio denounces Cordova, 24 years, eight of whom lived on the ridge of theAnti-Mafia, author of "land sold" for the types of Laruffa, where traces of the shame "landfill of Italy", by Pertusola in Crotone (establishment of a public companydisposed of) the dump of Motta San Giovanni, Reggio out where—as established bythe DDA Reggio—Iamonte family (almost all arrested on July 11, Crime in the transaction) had buried one hundred thousand tons of toxic waste, sludge and oilresidues from the combustion of a thermoelectric power station of Enel Brindisi. One hundred thousand tons of hazardous waste, Gian Luca Ursini notes on "PeaceReporter."

The 'ndrina poisoned water, air and land in Calabria for thirty years and now find theMilan magistrates, for 15 years so do the damage of "Lumbard". Stelvio, Valtellina, Como, Fair, Door: it seems to be at least in part to the current employees of the company Ivano Perego: the workers, continues Ursini, were intimidated by the thugs'ndrina, which actually belonged to the company. "The Strange picciotti Salvatore Platìbeat and threatened the workers with a minimum of scruples were realizing that to bury dangerous asbestos in the excavations of the work contracted by the General Contractor Perego, a modern name for scams and as old as the hills of death", saidUrsini.

The highway Stelvio in Valtellina, St. Anna Hospital in Como, the area "hatch" in Milan, the new "City Life" which is to supplant the old Fair in Milan, Lombardy, Padania, "all flooded toxic waste from the Mafia, "which continues to ignore it, untilthe poisoning" does not begin to kill people, "undermining the health." All around memy family, my neighbourhood, people are dying like flies, each family bereavement: what we have covered up for decades?". What John Nucera, animator of a cityhealth committee, is a desperate cry: Ravagnese the district of Reggio, behind the airport, the gangs have buried Books De Stefano and industrial waste in the 80s. Decades later, the bodies begin to collapse.

Between the time you ask Ursini, the 9 million Lombard find that cancer clusters in areas contaminated soar with abnormal indices of cancer patients, as for years in Calabria? "To allow the Mafia to break the rules mean to undermine your health, our investigations show," Cordova gloss. "As found in Valtellina is just the beginning:

the 'Ndrangheta has coached a long time 30 years ago and is now leveraging this expertise," explains Baldessarro: "The first investigations of this kind are of the late '80s." Cancer invading our tissues, whereas in those sites, "the works were done with filling Eternit asbestos and other toxic materials from demolition undifferentiated," confesses a worker to the magistrates.

According to the investigating judge, the waste, instead of being sorted anddisposed of in accordance with, were crushed at random and abandoned construction sites or illegal sites. "You begin to ask those who have worked in the dump truck in the home belonged to the company," Ursini insists on "Peace Reporter." Gennari for the magistrate, "the company Perego mobsters Strangio were directly involved in the work; in symbiosis between the Mafia and businesses." Ask yourself, concludes Ursini, who are the c ompanies that work under the house to see who refer: "The 'ndrina are among us, in your neighbourhood. Everywhere. To the north and south as we are killing everyone. Slowly".

And as always, the conclusion is always that, do you read already what is going on for so many years in Italy? What do you combine these stinking criminals? Am I right in claiming that in Veneto, there are venetian leaders, and not from the south? Yet there are a lot of venetian people still sleeping, and they does not realized what irreparable damage they continue to do the lords of the 'Ndrangheta in our Veneto. Now, unfortunately, due to the same Italian nationality can not expel them and restore legality.

But once born the Venetian Republic, you will need a lot of disinfectant, because for too many years, the gangs from the South are present in our area.

Let's now talk of toxic waste buried at sea by sinking ships full of cans, into the sea. The total lack of fight against organized crime in southern Italy, by Italian governments of the past, has produced rotten and corrupt society, which now, withhuge costs, it seems, now the Italian government is trying to counter, it's late Unfortunately the irreparable damage to the environment has been produced. The problem is very serious . . .

The secret services, paid bosses to sink the ships of poisons

Infamous pact between the state and the 'Ndrangheta traffic of toxic waste

Reopen the investigation on the murder of Ilaria Alpi and death of the consultant's Attorney of Reggio Calabria, De Grazia.

Behind the criminal trafficking of toxic waste on which the spotlight has reignited the investigation of the prosecutor Paola Giordano Bruno, lurks a real Mafia criminal conspiracy involving the highest political and state institutions and intelligence, theinner sanctum of the 'Ndrangheta of Calabria, Masons and unscrupulous wheeler, in the second half of '80, in exchange for kickbacks they planned to swirling around the sinking of "at least thirty ships" loaded with poisons from processing waste from thelarge factories of the north Italy disposed along the Mediterranean coast of Somalia, and with catastrophic consequences for the people and the whole environment.

Not only. Among the papers there are also links the investigation to the murder of Ilaria Alpi, the TG3 journalist killed along with his cameraman Miran Hrovatin 20 March 1994 in Somalia, perhaps because he had discovered something unspeakabletruth about the massive arms smuggling and toxic waste elapsed between Italy and Somalia during the imperialist military occupation called "Operation ibis."

The statements of "regret", Francesco Fonti

A repeat was the former boss of the 'Ndrangheta, Francesco Fonti, who among other things, with its revelations made it possible to discover, on Sept. 12, the wreckof the "Cunski" sunken ship from the same sources, and other 'Ndrangheta, with a volley of dynamite in 1992, to 11.8 nautical miles off the coast of Cetraro (Cosenza) exactly at the point indicated by the repentant. Sources, in fact, talking about the disposal of toxic waste in Somalia has said that this was done through the use ofships of the company Shifco. A name, this is closely linked to the murder of the Alps and Hrovatin. Especially since his last journey to Bossaso in the TG3 journalist had interviewed the Sultan of the place, Bogor Abdullahy Mussa, asking insistentlydetailed information on their fleet of fishing boats and ships which lay behind theShifco.

But that's not all: Wells, who currently is not subject to any protection regime and isunder house arrest, said to have directly participated in the sinking of three ships in the sea in Calabria, the Cunsky, which could be detected in Cetraro, the Yvonne A, and Voriais, but to have known, that the overall sinking boats made by the 'Ndrangheta, with their loads of waste, "are over thirty."

"It was an easy procedure and routine. I said and I repeat that in total tranquility on the seabed of Calabria there are about 30 ships. I've had sunk three, but each yearto the shrine of cuffs (province of Reggio Calabria), the plenary meeting was held of the 'Ndrangheta, where the heads stick summarizing activities in their territories. on these occasions, I heard it described the sinking of at least three ships in the area between Scylla and Charybdis, the other from Tropea, the other still close in Croton. And do not push me over for not being imprecise."

The Involvement of Intelligence Services

Rather high accuracy, Fonti, uses it when it rebuilds the system that governed the disappearance of ships at the bottom of the Mediterranean and the colossal deal of toxic waste by calling into question the political and institutional leaders of the time and intelligence.

My filter with the world of politics has been, since 1978, an agent of SISMI, which appeared under the name Pino. An athletic Thirty-year-old, about five feet tall with brown hair neatly combed back, introduced to me in capital by Guido Giannettino (the agent involved in the coup of Sid in the Borghese and the Piazza Fontana massacre ed) at the end of the sixties had to tear trying to woo the hierarchy information of the 'Ndrangheta. It worked like this: the agent contacted Pino from the De Stefano clan in Reggio Calabria, who informed my boss Romeo, who in turn made me go to the Palace Hotel in Rome, in Via Nazionale. From there I phoned the secretary of the SISMI (military secret internal service), saying, "I'm talking to Ciccio and Pino." Then I was called them at their hotel number and the meeting took place. The agent Pino told me the amount of waste that we had to get rid of and asked me if we could act immediately. It was a great deal, starting at 4 billion lire (over €2 million) for a load of old and coming up to a maximum of 30 billion lire (over €15 million). The money was paid on time in Lugano, either at the Whisky Agency on behalf of the bank, at the UBS Airport, or in some banks in Cyprus, Malta, Vaduz, and Singapore. All operators engaged in secrecy thanks to the advice of banker Valentino Foti, with which we had a cynical relationship of mutual convenience.

The Role of Government

As for the politicians who supported the agent, Pino's sources revealed the following:

> I met several times with Riccardo Misasi to handle the trafficking and disappearance of hazardous waste. This was the strong man for the Christian Democrats in Calabria, who told us whether the loads should be buried or sunk in Italian territory or foreign. The 'Ndrangheta, in fact, had sunk ships off the coast of Kenya, Somalia, and Zaire (formerly the Belgian Congo), using Italian captains and mixed crews of Europeans with Tunisians, Moroccans, and Albanians . . . Most of the ships were made to disappear at the bottom of our seas, and not just around the Calabria but also off the coast of La Spezia and Livorno, where I Iamonte Cristiano said that he had "arranged" a load of toxic waste in a drug's affair of the north.

That's not all. According to the repentant Mr. Fonte, another prominent politician had a role in the big business of hazardous waste. "This is the former Secretary of the DC Ciriaco De Mita, who was implicated by Misasi in the early eighties as the first person to care for the price of disposal required by the State. We met three or four times with De Mita in his apartment in Rome, and we agreed upon disposal fees." When this was completed,

> the agent Pino noted that the bank where we could go and collect the money, which had been credited to the accounts of Mr. Michael Sita, a false name on

my fake documents. Even the cars that I used to go to recover the money I gave it directly with the mediation of SISMI agent Pino. To protect myself from the threat of attack, I marked the type of machines and the freshmen were on diplomatic documents . . . In one case I drove an armored Fiat Croma with the serial VL In 7214, CD-11-01, in another, I drove an Audi with the serial BG 146-791, and in yet another, I traveled in a Mercedes with the serial BG 454-602. Needless to say, we were assigned diplomatic car suffered because border controls . . . I went, recovered the cash, and gave it to the family in Romeo St. Luca, where I received my share: about 20 per cent of the total.

The Investigations and Cover Up

The conditions of the case had been laid out twelve years earlier, in the first investigation of toxic waste dumping, initiated by Attorney General of the Court of Appeals of Reggio Calabria Francesco Neri, who had already attempted to find the wreckage, asking Minister of Justice Mancuso for a hundred million lire (€50,000). This was enough just to verify points on a map of the Mediterranean, as well as the names of ships, dates of sinking, and ship registry numbers. This painstaking detective work was led by Commander Natale De Grazia as a consultant to the Prosecutor of Reggio Calabria, who died mysteriously on 12 December 1995, after drinking a cup of coffee (as Sindona did) at a highway rest stop in Lower Nocera (Salerno) as he was on his way to La Spezia from Reggio Calabria to collect important documents for the case. Requests for further funds to continue the investigation were denied, and the investigation was shelved.

The Role of Fixer Comerio

The commander De Grazia reconstructed the routes that the ships carrying the hazardous materials followed. In particular he investigated the *Riegel*, sunk in 1987 in the Ionian Sea, and the *Jolly Rosso, Amantea* beached before 14 December 1990. Right in the cockpit of *JollyRosso*. De Grace discovered a map of sites for the sinking, the same one that would be found five years later in the home of Di Giorgio Comerio, the Italian wheeler in the middle of a series of events related to Somalia and the illegal aid management of the Directorate General for Economic Cooperation and Development. That is the engineer who—according to several investigations by both parliamentary prosecutors—would be the link between the case of ships of poisons, Somalia, and cooperation. Comerio participated in the "Dodos" conceived by ISPRA (the Institute for Environmental Research and Protection Agency), in which it planned to plunge radioactive materials stowed in torpedo warheads to the bottom of the sea. Following the conclusion of a UN convention that prevented the spillage of hazardous material on the seabed, the project was abandoned by ISPRA but not by Comerio. The fixer fact acquires the rights of the technology and signing an agreement with theSomali government $5 million, which expects to plunge radioactive waste off the coast. In return, pay €10,000 for each tangent to the sinking of the winning faction leader Ali Mahdi era. Finally, Comerio went around to the world's governments proposing to dispose of hazardous waste at discounted prices and get dozens of orders in black.

De Grazia probably had discovered everything, including the ports of departure of the waste, almost all located between Tuscany and Liguria, where there are two very favourable conditions: the military area of La Spezia and the marble quarries of the Apuan Alps: the first provides discretion, and the second provides the granules of marble with which to cover the emissions of radioactive waste. And that day, says a colleague of De Grazia, "We were going to La Spezia to verify the shipping register, which contained the names of about 180 ships sunk in suspicious ways in recent years and start from that area."

That's why now, in light of what has revealed the mafia repented Mr. Fonte, the Civic Committee, called Natale De Grazia, calls for the reopening of the murder case of Mr. Natale De Grazia. Now, said a representative of the committee, "it's time to go through and discover the whole truth."

Since the 90s there had been suspicions that ships full of radioactive waste were being sunk at sea. This is not only the fault of the Italian government but of all governments. In all countries, governments should monitor the destination of toxic waste. Unfortunately, in a country like Italy, so full of criminal organizations willing to do anything for money, you cannot leave this in the hands of the people. The government should be in control, but instead there was always someone with the toxic waste we wanted to earn. It has a beautiful telling of that astute Saviano, who were the industrial north to pollute. The industrial north produced waste, it is true, but those who damaged the environment were your people, perhaps your own neighbors, for those of you who live in Naples. In other European countries, this does not happen, because they do not have the south of Italy as part of their country. Let me explain. Suppose that in 1860, we moved to northern Italy, to Tuscany and allowed the Swedes to join Italy. After decades, you would see that they too behaved like the industrial North. This is true even for the Germans and other European countries. However, we have seen in the North the immigration of the Mafia, Camorra, and 'Ndrangheta. So sneaky, to play the victim and the hero because no one in your country knows these things, not even the children.

You need to come off that pedestal you've built in cooperation with RAI executives and other characters. The facts speak for themselves. Criminal organizations are born in the south, invented by the people of the south, not us from the north. We are so naive that even today we allow wise guys from the south to occupy positions in our regional governments, because it is a tradition in the south, have diplomas or degrees with very high ratings in order to help people win competitions in any field of public administration in the country. This dishonesty that is in the south of the country is known to all by now, but unfortunately despite that, this disgusting way of cheating goes on without stopping, indeed, ignorant of northern Italy they moved to the south, to obtain a degree.

In fact, when I see the people of the North, listening to the amazing stories they tell, I see myself a few years ago, when I did not know the history of the Italian people and their cultural differences. You, Saviano, as a good Southerner, banks on naiveté and ignorance of others. So many, like me, simply change the channel when they see people like you on TV, since wise guys like you now fill their sets.

The facts speak for themselves. Italian jails more than a third filled with foreigners, while those from the North do not account for even 10 per cent. Milan, Turin, and Genoa are southern cities, because they consist of 80 per cent or more from the south. You have a lot of nerve to blame the Piedmont of 150 years ago for your misfortune and poverty. Things must have been great for you in the past, because you have been content for the last fifty years not to move forward.

I see that in my country, Veneto, people have rolled up their sleeves, worked, and refuse to cry for money from the State like you do. Dodger, a Saviano, connected to the Internet and opens the Web on the 1980 Irpinia earthquake. Read the Wikipedia page or the many books written about the scandals and robberies that took place in the aftermath of the earthquake, which cost the State until now more than €66 billion. More than twenty books have been written about the scandals.

You can start by checking the Wikipedia page on the earthquake in Friuli-Venezia-Giulia in 1976. Read carefully to see how many scandals occurred in Irpinia, near your home, in your Campania. Then see how many books have been written about unimaginable fraud against the State perpetrated by the citizens it Friuli? *No one.* I hope that Saviano has the opportunity for reflection and self-criticism, because, his interview on RAIUNO at 20 pm during newsline

I have not digested. His accusation against the industrial of the north of the country, which according to him, are the cause of the huge illegal disposal of toxic waste in southern Italy. As if any person from the north, could go in the south, to discharge, waste wherever it wants. Even children know that nothing happens in the southwithout the consent of the mafia, then Saviano, please start talking seriously, because of stupid things you've already said enough in that interview.

It happened a few years ago, it is true, but it still sits in my stomach, as a citizen of the North, who is offended to see people go on national TV, which I pay for with my annual fees, and makes such assertions.

March 2010: To provide raise awareness among those who do not know the people of the South, Saviano fixed this article:

Let's go back to writing about the poison ships, full of toxic waste, and left to sink into the Tyrrhenian Sea in southern Italy in the mid-80s you knew what was happening. If we had had serious governments, however, governments of criminals, you probably would have intervened first and stop these criminals, who in my opinion, deserve the penalty death. It is unthinkable to show compassion to those who know no mercy. Here there is some more news:

In 1985, while traveling from La Spezia to Lome (Togo), the ship *Nikos* disappeared, probably between Lebanon and Greece. In 1985 the German ship *Koraline* sank off the coast of Ustica. In 1986 it was the turn of the *Mikigan*, sailing from the port of Marina di Carrara in the Tyrrhenian Sea and sinking with its suspicious Calabrian cargo. In 1987, twenty miles from Cape Teulada in Calabria, the *Rigel* was shipwrecked. In 1989, the Maltese ship *Years of Ravenna* sank in international waters. In 1990, it was the turn of the *Jolly Red* beached along the Tyrrhenian coast in the province of Cosenza. In 1993, the *Marco Polo* disappeared in the Sicilian Channel.

In October 2008, the president of the Calabria region, Agazio Loiero, in a meeting with Interior Minister Maroni (Northern League Party), the Director of ANAS (road governmental entity), and the president of Confindustria, Emma Marcegaglia, explained the problems that the 'Ndrangheta procuring was, during the construction of the Salerno-Reggio Calabria Highway. He was very worried, saying that Calabrian crime makes life impossible for companies like Impregilo and Astaldi, whose construction sites had been targeted by ninety attacks and intimidation of various kinds in the last year. "At this point I wonder if the government, so attentive to the problems of security, also recognizes that of organized crime. I also wonder why the work on the highway never ends, if not for the interests and pressures of gangs." As you know by now, the 'Ndrangheta forces firms to buy from them the materials to be used in the construction of roads, material often mixed with toxic waste.

The study I've done is enough to make a concerned citizen pull out his hair. A just punishment for these Mafia criminals would be hard labor until death. Alas, the imbeciles who claim to support human rights would never allow this to happen. They will carry on to slip through the sieve of justice, and we Italians will all be in terrible shape.

Chapter 14

But What Kind of Country We Are Talking About?

Let's just see what kind of country we are talking about:

- A country, very corrupt, in which there is an unacceptable law(prescription) that say 10 years after the 'beginning of the process, if not concluded, the process must be canceled permanently.
- A country where the politician Giulio Andreotti, although it confirmed the crime of conspiracy, not convicted because prescribed, is still a senator for life.
- The country whose head of state, Giorgio Napolitano, has for decades left his fellow citizens and voters of Naples wallowing in garbage and allowed the Camorra (organized crime) to dictate laws in the territory.
- A country where the Prime Minister, Silvio Berlusconi, allows his government to be populated by corrupt people like him.
- A country where there are 629,120 cars provided by the various state agencies, regions and provinces throughout Italy paid with taxpayers money(data of May 2010). But w, e're kidding?
- A country made up of two very different ethnic groups of peoples, with totally unequal cultures.
- A country that for decades has allowed Chinese entrepreneurs to import low-cost labor from their country, resulting in the loss, in Prato (Tuscany) alone, of more than 10,000 jobs, not to mention the rest of the jobs lost throughout Italy.
- A country that has never critically fought organized crime.
- A country that has never seriously fought tax evasion.
- A country that has never had a respect for its citizens (for example, the Venetians).
- A country that, from the 60s onwards, has continued to let its financial system collapse.

A country that, for decades, has allowed doctors and nurses to practise the profession although unable, because they bought their degree or diploma, killing thousands of people in hospitals throughout Italy, especially in the south.,.

- A country that has in the past allowed govrnment's workers to retire after fifteen years and six months, while other employees had to work for thirty-five years.
- A country whose public schools have 1 janitor for every 2.5 classes.

- A country that pays employees of the House and Senate more than anywhere else in the world.
- A country that pays its deputies and senators more than in any other democratic country in the world.
- A country in which most politicians differ greatly in their culture and ways of thinking from the people who built and enriched the country.
- A country where the Parliament begins work on Tuesday morning and goes home on Thursday afternoon.
- A country whose governmental department in its capital, Rome, has more than 4,000 officers.
- A country where Ms Irene Pivetti, former President of the Chamber of Deputies (from April 1994 to May 1996), for life, it will have the car and bodyguards, provided by the State, always at your service.
- A country where the Constitutional Court judges retire at 12,000 Euros net per month, are entitled to car and driver, paid by the State, until their deaths.
- A country in which the Italian government costs more than the governments of France, Germany and England combined.
- A country whose economy is being choked by high taxes, because corrupt politicians have never had the will to resolve the issue of the South, which is slowing down the whole country.
- A country where some regions will allow you to run up debts which are then paid by the state, with everybody's money.
- A country where politicians' salaries are unequal across regions to the point where in Sicily they are double than those of Veneto
- A country where you need to wait ten years to receive justice in cases where you are in the right, and that's if you're lucky.
- A country in which all public procurement of major works is awarded for bribes and costs three to four times more than in other European countries.
- A country that for over forty years has allowed private hospitals to defraud the National Healt, for example with billing for services never rendered.
- A country that, thirty-one years after investigating a plane shot down in Ustica, no one knows by whom, has been ordered to pay compensation of €100 million to relatives of eighty-one victims. The court of Palermo has also accused the ministries of the state of covering up the truth by providing false leads and destroying evidence. A country where radar picked up no traces of evidence.
- A country that for decades has had millions of civil servants for electoral reasons only.
- A country that in public administration, as honesty is at 67° place in the world.
- A country where success in government departments requires one to be cunning and corrupt.
- A country that, despite the outbreak of Tangentopoli in 1992, thanks to the pool of Milan, managed to make a clean sweep of corrupt politicians yet saw everything go back to the way it was before.

- A country that, instead of assisting Operation Clean Hands, saw its two opposing political coalitions (Berlusconi on one side and Olive on the left) deploy together to promote laws that would help the politicians involved in corruption get out as soon as possible.
- A country that has always passed laws to encourage tax evaders, as in the case of the law decriminalizing false accounting.
- A country where corruption in public administration grew in 2010 by 30 per cent, costing to the Italian government 60 billions Euros per year instead of 40.
- A country that has made corruption a way of life.
- A country that oppresses the people of the north to maintain a lazy and spendthrift South.
- A country in which young people cannot find work because it allows businesses and individuals to employ foreigners badly paid at €3 or €4 per hour.

What I have written above is not intended to create hatred for the people of the South. Indeed, it is the right of every country to place its decision-making powers in the hands of its own people. To do anything otherwise is absolutely unfair, as is unfortunately the case in our Veneto region, where Southerners have invaded all public areas. Venetians, take back your dignity as a people. Too many people died in the Veneto region a century and a half ago so that the people of Veneto would be respected as a people. Do not forget the sacrifices of our ancestors when the referendum is held to refund the republic of Venice. Together we can vote *yes* to pay homage to our ancestors and regain our freedom and dignity, something we lack today.

I'm not the only one to speak about the evil of the South. Let's hear what Daniela Minerva, in her book La fiera dlla sanità *(The Fair Health)*, had to say in 2009, not 50 years ago!

> And have generated an Italy split, with citizens from Veneto, Emilia Romagna, Friuli, but not only, in full control of their health care institutions and aims to ensure that they function as clocks, and other adrift, hopeless and victims of political, robbers, trade unionists and even prelates, who not only are they deprived of a right, but also the dignity of work in the medical and paramedical staff, appointed to ensure that the right is respected. What hurts, Cardarelli Hospital in Naples, or at the Polyclinic hospital of Rome, is not only the neglect and abandonment . . . is seeing patients waiting for treatment, or even information, a grace as if they were.

In many large hospitals in the south, consisting of many buildings, there is no signage on how to reach a particular department, however, paying 10 euros to the clerk or nurse that you encounter on the street, you have solved the problem. One thing like that in Verona, it would cause a pandemonium.

Ignazio Marino, a surgeon and senator of the Democratic Party made the following statements:

147

1. It is true that in 2007, Prodi pushed through a law in Parliament to use the money of all Italians to revoke the debts of regions heavily indebted in health (remember the hoard of €11 billion?), as always, from the South. Well, after rescheduling the debts, southern regions continued to mount up debts (while continuing to defraud the healthcare system in the South). Marino blames incompetent CEOs hired for their allegiance to a party instead of their ability.

2. The journalist poses this inquiry to Senator Marino: "If a virtuous alteration was possible in Veneto and Emilia-Romagna, this happened because in those parts of the country, there was strong social cohesion and a sense of individual responsibility. What are the fuels of the National Health Service: where do not exist, it does not have the energy they need to live. But in many parts of Italy, the social fabric is very different." This question, from what I read, the senator responded by saying that in the south because health is malfunctioning, "is related to the different cultures of Italy". Senator was clear!

The following data was reported by Professor Luke Ricolfi, currently a columnist for the newspaper *La Stampa* of Turin. He is also a teacher of Psychometrics at the Faculty of Psychology, University of Turin. He has written more than a dozen books and essays, including *The Bag of the North*.

D	Rate Evasion
Lombardia	12.5%
Emilia Romagna	19.0%
Veneto	19.6%
Friuli Venezia Giulia	24.7%
Lazio	25.0%
Piemonte	26.1%
Trentino Alto Adige	26.2%
Media Italiana	**26.4%**
Toscana	27.6%
Valle d'Aosta	27.6%
Marche	28.0%
Abruzzo	30.5%
Umbria	37.5%
Liguria	42.3%
Basilicata	48.4%

Molise	50.9%
Sardegna	51.3%
Puglia	52.0%
Campania	55.3%
Sicilia	63.4%
Calabria	85.3%

According to Professor Ricolfi, the statistics are shocking because the allocation of tax evasion is a bit different from that to which He's got used to a certain vulgate. When it comes to tax evasion, Lombardy and Veneto are the first and third most honourable regions, thus disproving the vulgate, who wants to portray Lombardy-Veneto as a land of tax evaders. In fact, Lombards and Venetians have been pushing for aggressive taxation against the state vampire, paying their taxes regularly. To the north, the more "naughty" turn out to be residents in the red regions (Emilia Romagna excluded).

But the actual gap is still in the south. Among the regions in central and southern Lazio is only to be below the Italian average, probably because of the very high percentage of government employees living in Rome and province. Rounding out the rankings are the three regions Ricolfi called "regions of the Mafia", or Campania, Sicily, and Calabria. Logic would dictate that if you really needed to step up the fight against tax evasion, you would intensify your efforts where there was a greater chance of improvement, namely under the Gothic Line.

From the website *Lawyers without Borders:*

Judiciary Contest Tricks: Are they controlled by Mafia Judicial and Camorra?

Maybe it's just one of many outlandish anomalies, perhaps an Italian phenomenon of patriotism, perhaps a most alarming sign of the widespread control of the Mafia of the future structure of the judiciary to avoid the annoying problem of judges not aligned to the interests of massomafie.

The Ministry of Justice, on their website, released the official list of candidates admitted to the oral contest for 350 seats in the judiciary, announced 15 December 2009. From the list, unless we have counted wrong, we learned that 343 aspirants will face the next oral examinations. The final data are as follows:

Naples, the capital of the Camorra, is also the capital of promotions: of 343 oral exams, 180 are admitted to Naples, 110 to Sicily, and many to Rome.

Meanwhile, the Courts of Appeal of Turin and Florence have churned out a number of judges equal to 0 (zero), while Milan has 2.

Why?

Is not that the commission is composed mostly of judges and professors of Neapolitan origin?

I would like to note that the website *Lawyers without Borders* is not affiliated with any political party. What this website explains tells us a lot about what is happening across the country. Is it wrong for lawyers of Veneto to complain that their courts are no longer Venetian?

MASSOMAFIE: query for SAVIANO, AND NAPOLITANO HAS NO ANSWER;

Here is a parliamentary matter a few years ago still very current on the existence of massomafie that nobody talks about. Even Saviano. The present anew entirety noting that went unanswered, curiously when the current President of the Neapolitan Republic was Minister of the Interior.

To the Minister of the Interior, for the coordination of civil protection,

Given:

- That the recent news stories have revealed a serious situation of collusion between members of law enforcement agencies operating in Campania Camorra and environments; this involves agents and police officers who were also members of secret associations;
- That Minister Napolitano, referring to the situation, said he was ready to take any necessary action to remedy it;
- That the citizens of Naples react by showing a deep mistrust of the institutions, because, according to a survey by the CIRM company, on behalf of the newspaper *"TheMorning "*,60 per cent of the Neapolitan believes that the Camorra will never be defeated. While the prosecutor Agostino Cordova, expressed during an interview with *Corriere della Sera newspapier*, that he believes in some districts of Naples, the Camorra controls not only the State but also argues that if there are leaks in the police, it is the fault of Ministry of the Interior officials;
- On this occasion it is right to note that even in the north, there is a deep disregard for law enforcement and the judiciary, the Camorra organized crime and Mafia-style implanted dangerous financial centre's devoted to money laundering through the management of each type of industrious goings-on;
- That for decades Milan has been neglected in each survey (an example for everyone on the fleet of Solomon), but also for some time Turin, Venice, who Cortina d'Ampezzo is one of the places chosen as venues for major bases of the Mafia thanks to dozens of corporations, financial, real estate, construction companies and even airlines, the phenomenon is of

such magnitude as to involve some banks that manage bank accounts of companies linked to the Camorra and the Mafia, according to the old, but you always see valid principle that "money through does not smell";

- That the Camorra Mafia and 'Ndrangheta from the south are the primary threat to liberty and security of citizens of the North, and that the arrival of too many Southerners, as leaders of the police and ordinary police in the north, has facilitated the penetration of these mafias.

Conclusion

I repeat again for undecided people, who do not feel it is right to separate Veneto from Italy:

Dear fellow Venetians, from the 60s onwards, the south has had rivers of money to develop their territory. If their politicians used the money to organize parties and community work that produced nothing, how is this the fault of Veneto? In short, the people of Veneto have done their duty, but if the populations in the south just have a different culture, what are we to do? Should we succumb to them? How far must solidarity go for its own sake?

Venetians, once and for all, let's be realistic. I too, until a few years ago, was naïve and did not know the facts, but now that I have opened my eyes I cannot help but come to this conclusion. Let's forget about all the various parties who have contributed to this Italian disaster. Let's allow the Venetian people to decide their own future, not Rome. We must have a Republic of Venice that is commanded by Venetians. All the injustices enumerated above would never happen in the nation of Veneto.

We must be masters of our own house, because Veneto is *our country*.

Here is why Bossi should have organized a referendum to divide the country in 1995:

- If Italy had been divided in two in 1995, southern Italian would have rolled up its sleeves and start working, or drowned in the deepest misery.
- With the division, Southern fraud against the Italian state would have ended.
- The South would not have been able to get money from the government of Rome (because northern Italy would no longer be supporting her). Southerners would finally have to work in the world, since the INPS and other organizations would be bankrupt without northern money. As such there would be a dramatic decrease of false illness and accidents in the factories and fields.
- The honest people of the South would have put the bad ones in line. Having little money available, everyone would be obliged to work well with the little they had, instead of stealing from hospitals and other institutions as if they were banks to be robbed.
- Having little money, the South would not have allowed illegal immigration to run wild, because the illegal immigrants they would have stolen your place of work.
- Having divided Italy, we in the North would have governments that are closer to their citizens and businesses, with a government in Milan or some other city

153

instead of a legion of Roman bureaucrats to which we are slaves. In this way we could have reduced taxes, we would not have so many illegal immigrants, and we would not be plagued with gangs from the South.

Several years have passed since 1945. Many say that you cannot change the constitution, that Italy is one and indivisible. Those who say this belong in the asylum, as does President Napolitano. Dear Bossi, you should have held a referendum splitting the country. Now it may be too late, and the damage is incalculable. In 1995 the people of the south would have had ample time to modify their ways of life. Now, facing economic crisis, the hardships will be immense. Since the 60s they have had the same opportunities as the North; the biggest difference is in the culture. The facts speak for themselves.

Dear Mr. Bossi, a representative from the financial police in the South once said, "you know the difference between the North and the South? Here in the North, I issue two or three fines, and I know that they will be paid immediately. In the South, I can write a hundred fines, and not a single one gets paid. This is not a joke. This is the reality."

This simple history book will be sure to offend many people in Italy. Nevertheless, the undersigned is pissed off, very pissed off about what happened in the past and what is still happening today. My country is locked into a terrible political marriage because of a scam, which was perpetrated 146 years ago. The culture of my country—Veneto—is as similar to regions such as such as Campania, Sicily, and Calabria as England or Germany is to Morocco or even China for that topic. I believe that every person should be the master of his own home. I am sick (and I am not alone—the Northern League is proof of this) of seeing the most infamous people in the country hold positions of public office in my Veneto, knowing the laziness, arrogance, and malice the southern people (not all, but many).

In order to unite the world, people must be open to make a decision with regard their own future. Until now this does not happen in Italy. No one wishes for divorce, but there is no other way to win the liberty of the peoples of the north.